Swimming Coaching

SWIMMING COACHING

Joseph Dixon

The Crowood Press

First published in 1996 by
The Crowood Press Ltd
Ramsbury, Marlborough
Wiltshire SN8 2HR

This impression 2000

British Library Cataloguing in Publication Data
A catalogue record for this book is available from the
British Library

ISBN 1 85223 998 0

Picture Credits:
All photographs by the author

Acknowledgements:
My grateful thanks are due to the following people whose help and
consideration were always available: Doctor Moira O'Brien, FRCPI
of the Anatomy Department, Trinity College, Dublin; Professor Craig Sharp,
Professor of Sports Science at Limerick University; Andy Kerr, BAWLA
senior coach; Tony Carney at the Department of Psychiatry, Clinical Science
Institute UCH Galway, and the chief coach at the Laser ASC Galway;
John O'Connor BLC, solicitor in Dublin; Roy Romain, Olympian and international
swimmer; John Cardwell, international and PE instructor at the British
Police Federation; 'Paddy' Hayes, ASA coach who coached five Olympic
swimmers and never quite received the recognition he fully deserved; Trojan
ASC, Blackrock, Dublin; and finally Kings Hospital ASC, Palmerstown, Dublin.

Thanks also to the following swimmers for their efforts and to those whose
photographs appear in this book: Vanessa Bagot, Amersham ASC; Nicola Coffey,
Amersham ASC; Rebecca Dickinson, Bodmin ASC; Siobhan Doyle, Trojan ASC,
Cathy Finlay, Guildford City ASC; Aofie Fitzgerald, Trojan ASC; Brian Harris, Trojan ASC;
Ciaran Kirby, Kings Hospital ASC; David Kitterick, Torjan ASC; Rachel Lee,
Kings Hospital ASC; Ciaran McGrath, Trojan ASC; Niall Moraghan, Trojan ASC;
Sally O'Herlihy, Trojan ASC; Conor Osborough, Trojan ASC; Nikki Ramsey,
Guildford City ASC; Daragh Sharkey, Trojan ASC

Dedication:
To Rita, for her patience and understanding, and for always being there.

Printed and bound by Redwood Books, Trowbridge.

Contents

Preface

The author was previously the swimming development officer for the Leinster branch of the Irish Amateur Swimming Association. He has tutored many courses, and was responsible for the considerable development of swimming skills, particularly at the lower levels. He wrote a manual, *Swimming Organisation,* on how to set up and manage a swimming club which would enable teachers, coaches and swimmers to achieve a much higher standard of knowledge and expertise. *Swimming Organisation* covered these areas in considerable detail. His latest book, *Swimming Coaching,* is written in simple language and generously illustrated with high quality underwater photographs. It is a comprehensive book which covers all aspects of swimming and in particular reveals his considerable knowledge regarding the techniques of stroke, starts and turns. Irish swimming is indebted to the author both for his contribution to swimming in Leinster and for this very fine book on swimming.

Fergus Barron
President of the Irish Amateur
Swimming Association

'Whatever you do in swimming requires courage and a belief in yourself, for whatever course you choose to adopt will be commented upon by some expert who will always state it is wrong. The funny thing was, my swimmers continued to get faster in spite of the fact the things I did were wrong.'

Paddy Hayes, coach to four
Olympians and international swimmers

Introduction

Swimming Coaching is a book which I hope will enable swimmers and swimming coaches, not only in the UK but the world over, to achieve higher standards of knowledge and expertise in every aspect of this skilful and exciting sport. The wealth of information it contains is also, I hope, presented in text and photographs which readers will find clear, concise and easy to understand and assimilate.

The introduction of the National Training Centre qualifications in Ireland and NVQs (National Vocational Qualifications) in the UK has brought about a certain merging of teaching and coaching practices in swimming; in view of this development, each chapter in this book provides updated information regarding the latest techniques of stroke, starts and turns, information which will be found invaluable for any swimming syllabus. The description of each technique is accompanied by drills, the purpose for those drills and the relevant teaching and coaching points. Information relevant to the various swimming courses offered by clubs and associations throughout the UK has been compiled in depth and also included here.

Underwater photography has always held a fascination for me, particularly as I believe that the true meaning of certain points in technique is sometimes lost when presented in a diagram, usually because the artist fails to comprehend the principles of water. Moreover a clear photograph with a good technical back-up is far more informative than many pages of in-depth explanation. My knowledge of underwater photography has been put to good use in several books (John Verrier's *Swimming*, David Sparkes' *Swimming For All* and Helen Elkington's very good work on synchro to name but three), and here, too, it is put to great effect in the 200 or so photographs and illustrations which help clarify the detailed descriptions of the techniques presented in this edition. It is hoped that these explanations, together with the many photographs of the strokes, starts, turns and takeovers described, will fully satisfy the needs and ambitions of swimmers and swimming coaches of all standards.

On numerous courses in Great Britain and Ireland, the principles of hydromechanics were taught in close association with the mechanical principles of the strokes, starts, turns and takeovers. This was singularly successful and the same formula has been adopted in this book. It is almost impossible to evaluate precisely the advantages of good start and turn techniques; the only arbiters are a coach's knowledge and the stop-watch. A common mistake is to concentrate on the start and turn alone, and pay scant attention to the approach and the transition into the stroke.

The starts and turns covered in this book have been thoroughly investigated, and this has created a new awareness of what can be accomplished with a more thoughtful and creative approach. Changes in the competition laws have made differences in seconds rather than in tenths of seconds, and there is room for still more improvement as techniques develop. At times we wait and learn from outside sources, rather than discovering for ourselves; for example the information concerning physiology has been updated using a methodology that we hope makes this complicated aspect easier to understand.

A teacher or a coach will go through progressive stages of accomplishment before a degree of confidence and satisfaction is attained. Usually we are introduced to the sport either as a competitor or a parent: as a competitor, the background has in many ways already been established; as a parent, the hunger for knowledge is usually greater. Knowledge is like a tunnel, and the curious will seek out information so the light at the end of the tunnel gets larger; by the time they emerge from the tunnel they are accomplished teachers and coaches. Others are less willing to accept and seek out new skills, and therefore restrict themselves to a lower level.

A swimmer may achieve success because he has a good teacher and coach who sets high standards in demonstrations, practices and logical coaching points. Other swimmers achieve success in spite of a teacher and coach with lower standards; in many scenarios, for instance, the only coaching point in start and turn practices is the word 'go', with no input of progressive preparation and teaching points which will improve the swimmer's skill.

The perfect balance of teaching and coaching will never be realized: a degree of parent power and a proportion of committee members will always ensure this. Any teacher and coach who feels maligned will always express the sentiment at one time or another that 'happiness is an orphan', and unfortunately Utopia in this sport is not possible.

In the last twenty-five years the sport of swimming has improved because of better coaching techniques, higher standards and changes in the laws of the sport. It is the striving for individual improvement in teaching and coaching methods and standards which will be responsible for continuing forward progress. So avoid moulding yourself on a particular personality, but adapt everything you find relevant to suit your own style of teaching and coaching. Make progress by utilizing information from every available source. And I hope that the information contained in this book will go a considerable way in helping you to attain your aspirations in this great sport of ours.

1

Principles and Hydromechanics

A dictionary defines a principle as 'a law concerning a natural phenomenon' or 'the behaviour of a system'. The definition of hydromechanics is 'the branch of science concerned with the mechanical properties of fluids, especially liquids. Also called hydrodynamics'. The main aim in this book is to present answers to many questions in a simplified manner; technical details have been elucidated with photographs and diagrams wherever possible. Constant reference is made throughout the book to the principles discussed in this chapter, and they are investigated in detail here to help the reader achieve an in-depth understanding of the various techniques. The following factors are linked to these techniques and the swimmer must consider them most carefully if he wants to go faster in water:

- Flotation and density
- Profile resistance
- Eddy current resistance
- Viscous drag resistance
- Streamlining and propulsion
- Propulsive stroke patterns

FLOTATION AND DENSITY ———

Both of these are individual characteristics. Women float better than men, but men are generally stronger in the arms and legs. In addition to this a man is normally larger in both height and in the size of his limbs (his 'levers'). The body is made up of muscle, skin and bone, some of which contribute to a degree of flotation in water. Body fats and air in the lungs are also responsible for the body being able to float; how well we do so depends on a delicate balance of the items in question. Nevertheless we cannot escape the fact that the mass of an element or body can only be interpreted as the density of that object.

All the swimmer can do to alleviate this problem of density is to use the lungs more efficiently, and time the breathing cycle precisely with that of the stroke cycle. The intake of oxygen is dictated by the stroke itself, and the accomplished swimmer adjusts both the inhalation and exhalation accordingly. In competitive swimming, all breathing is of a vigorous nature but the time taken to complete exhalation is greater than that taken to inhale. In a training environment more time is available in order to complete these phases in the breathing cycle. With the untutored or social type swimmer, the lack of correct breathing techniques is a contributing factor to a lower or an even more greatly inclined body position. In the initial stages of stroke improvement, not enough time and trouble is devoted to coaching the swimmer in breathing techniques and as a result lack of oxygen will most greatly inhibit his progress. Some swimmers in the early stages of stroke improvement tend to hold their breath and then exhale and inhale as one action but they accomplish it by breaking the rhythm of the stroke. In the front crawl stroke for example we often see an 'improving' type of swimmer 'over-roll' to breathe, so although the breathing cycle has been performed, it has led to the development of a major fault in technique. In this stroke most improvers speak of the difficulties they find in synchronizing breathing with that of the arm action. On land, breathing is a natural action and one that is accomplished without being taught. In water, it is imperative for the teacher and coach to spend

enough time correcting faults and improving this major function in the stroke.

PROFILE RESISTANCE

Progress through the water can be improved by reducing the resistance factors and by increasing the momentum by physical propulsion. A high level of technique and or an increase of repetitions in the stroke cycle results in even faster progress through water. Profile resistance will diminish as the body position improves and the swimmer achieves even greater confidence. His submerged profile will move a proportional mass of water ahead of him, so if he adopts an inclined body position there will be that much more water to move. But if he adopts a more streamlined position –

Fig 1a   Inclined body position and profile resistance.

Fig 1b   Efficiency in body streamlining.

stretched and parallel to the surface of the water – the resistance factor will be decreased and less water will have to be moved ahead of him. If swimmers are made aware of this principle, then greater speed and distance will be achieved.

EDDY CURRENT RESISTANCE ———

If a plank of wood is held upright in fast-moving water with its broader face turned against the flow, it will be difficult to hold it steady and 'swirls' will start to appear behind it. However, if the plank is turned side on so as to present the smaller area to the flow of water, holding it steady is much less of a problem and the 'swirls' or eddy currents will be seen to disappear. A poorly streamlined swimmer has the same effect in water: for example, if a front crawl swimmer flexes (dorsiflexes) the feet, eddy currents will be created behind the feet; but if he extends (plantar-flexes) the feet, the eddy currents will diminish.

This is also an important factor for the body as a whole in the turn for breast-stroke, butterfly, the 'throw-away' (front crawl) and fly to back medley turn. Thus if the swimmer turns 180 degrees from the wall, frontal resistance and eddy currents will be created; but if he turns just 90 degrees, the side of the body only will be presented before falling or 'knifing' into the water and away from the side, and this creates less resistance and eddy currents for the total action.

VISCOUS DRAG RESISTANCE ———

In swimming terms, 'viscosity' describes

Fig 2a   Tumble turn 'side-on' turning technique.

Fig 2b Breaststroke 'side-on' turning technique.

the extent to which a fluid resists its tendency to flow. A swimmer's body will create friction in the water by the very fact of the water molecules coming into contact with his skin; as he goes faster, so the level of friction – the viscosity – will increase. However, great improvements have been made in the materials used for swimming costumes; these have been developed to minimize the level of friction between water and the body of the swimmer. The level of friction is therefore less of a problem for the female swimmer, particularly as over the years, swim suits designed for the more competitive have attained the ultimate in tight, high-necked proportions thereby minimizing completely the 'funnel type' of resistance which existed in previous costume design. So both costume design and material very effectively minimize the effect of friction and frontal resistance. If this is an important consideration for the competitive swimmer, it is of huge advantage to the competitive female diver because when performing from the 10-metre platform, entry into the water at fast accelerating speed will create movement in even the tightest of swim-wear.

Viscosity is a greater problem for the male swimmer because a smaller area of his body is covered by costume. This can be counteracted to a degree by 'shaving down' for an important event. Shaving for an event undoubtedly has a stimulating effect, and as well as wearing a costume one size smaller, the feel of water

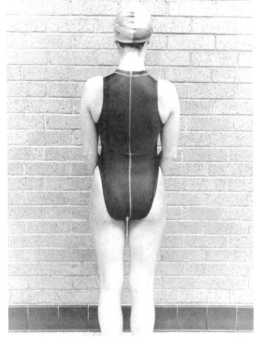

Fig 3a Front view of a type of costume which achieves the ultimate in low resistance for the competitive swimmer and diver.

Fig 3b Back view of the costume, creating low resistance in most areas of the body for the female competitve swimmer.

flow over the body and speed are both greatly enhanced.

HATS AND GOGGLES

Hats are essential in the reduction of resistance. They do, however, tend to 'furrow' owing to movement in water and should be adjusted tightly. Because of this they exert considerable pressure around the head, as do goggles; for this reason, a competitive swimmer at the end of a hard race will remove both his cap and goggles and immerse his head in the water to cool it down and so too the brain. It is a quick way towards recovery before 'swimming down' after an event.

STREAMLINING

The body can be considered as a set of levers which are programmed by the neuromuscular system. The main levers, in descending order of importance, are the head, upper trunk, upper leg, lower leg, feet, upper arm, lower arm and hands.

The levers of the body can be extended to achieve better streamlining, but they can also be flexed. The amount of angular flexion is of particular importance in achieving undulation for the teaching and coaching of the butterfly stroke.

If the levers of the body obtain full extension, then with a better technique in the leg action, the swimmer can attain an efficient body position. This encompasses three strokes, the front crawl, back crawl (during the complete stroke cycle of both strokes) and the breastroke at full extension.

Streamlining is also an important factor in both start and turn techniques; not only should the body be stretched but the arms should be close together with one hand on top of the other.

An efficient leg action not only contributes to propulsion, but in the leg kick downwards in both front crawl and back crawl the bearing surface area of the leg keeps the body high and facilitates the rolling action. In front crawl, if the action comes from the knee instead of the hip region, the knee will tend to 'vee' down into the water and this will have detri-

Fig 4 Good streamlining off the wall in the back crawl turn with one hand on top of the other.

Fig 5   Profile body resistance created by a 'vee' type of kick, where the action comes from the knee instead of the hip region.

mental results on the body position, the propulsive factor and longitudinal roll. If the kick is initiated at the knee in back crawl, the lower leg 'spears' downwards led by the heel, which again has a limiting effect on both propulsion and bearing area.

PROPULSION

Much has been written about propulsion in water. We have Newton's third law of motion, and there are parallelograms of forces with vertical, horizontal and resultant thrusts; velocities have been measured, and there is Bernoulli's principle of lift and drag and its resultants. The application of biomechanics in swimming has been both intriguing and stimulating. However, although these proofs and theories may be interesting and absorbing to some of us, for many, they are confusing.

We have come a long way from the 'push' and 'pull' theories of earlier years

– although when you consider it, are they that long ago? Some teachers and coaches still believe in these theories and put them into practice and certainly it appears to make sense that if a swimmer fixes on the water and pulls directly backwards, the body goes forwards. Newton's third law of motion tends to substantiate this: 'For every action there is an equal and opposite reaction.' When we fix onto something solid on land we can achieve the correct reaction; but water moves in the direction of the pressure. On coaching courses and seminars nowadays we are taught about the 'in sweep' and the 'out sweep' – but the synchro world has been preaching this, its only doctrine, since day one; although they, of course, always referred to it as 'sculling', which is its true meaning.

Not that long ago we had probably all heard of the American type of breaststroke as against the European type. However, it is food for thought that we never heard of the American type of sculling as against the European; or that the Pacific dolphin had a different propulsive principle from the European dolphin. But as long as the principles are understood, we should discover that there is a rational way in which to utilize the levers of the body in order to swim efficiently, and it is connected with the form that water takes, mainly in wave form. Thus in the outer sculling pattern we trace a wave-like path, and in the inner scull we trace an inverted wave-like pattern; connected together they form an 'S' formation (or a figure-of-eight cut down the middle). The outward sculling path is similar to an electrical sine wave which equates to two halves of a circle; since the circle adds up to 360 degrees, the principle must be that if we wish to fix efficiently in water, all movements should be circular.

The wave-like flow of water has also been taken into consideration in ship construction. In early designs, the bow of a ship always projected to cut sharply into the water; later, a 'bulbous' style became more common, with the water now flowing around the bow. It would be interesting to see the difference in resistance and speed factor if the hull, too, incorporated the same design ideas. Most fish and inhabitants of the sea move their fins up and down, or side to side; others perform a wave-like movement. If a strobe light were attached to the fin of any fish and activated, one would detect a wave-like pattern of light through the water. Similarly the up-and-down movements of the wings of any bird would trace out the same wave-like pattern.

For many centuries man has tried to fly like the birds, but although precision has been given to the wing structure, all attempts have ended in failure; one major reason for this is strength, since it has been established that the bird is approximately forty times stronger than man across the upper body. The dolphin can swim at speeds up to forty miles an hour (65kph), the fastest man can swim is about five miles per hour (8kph). Strength again is a dominant feature, as well as the fact that the dolphin is perfectly designed for its environment (interestingly, a model of a dolphin was once tested in a wind tunnel and aerodynamically it proved to be flawless). Evidently man evolved in the same environment but was equipped by nature to match his terrestrial surroundings: it is a simple fact, therefore, that he is no longer efficiently equipped for water. Swim he may, but to attain any speed in water he must use and train the levers of his body to a considerable level of efficiency; and the teacher and coach must have an in-depth understanding of water principles and the sculling patterns that should be related with them.

PROPULSIVE PATTERNS

The science of biomechanics has an in-depth explanation as to how forward progress is achieved through the movement of arms and legs, and in fact the Bernoulli principle of producing lift has been adopted in swimming and is used in all arm and leg movements. Many people find this difficult to follow precisely, and for them it is enough just to know that it actually works. For those who would like to understand the principle more clearly, however, the situation can be likened to a ship's propeller. The propeller blades on a ship are shaped, so as they turn they purchase a hold on to unturbulant, 'still' water and the ship then moves forwards by pole-vaulting or thrusting on this firm purchase. If the propeller had straight and not angularly shaped blades, the blades would not be cutting into 'still' water but would be rotating on water that was moving; thus it would be much harder for it to gain a purchase, and the ship would no longer move forwards readily (Fig 6).

The same principle can be applied to the hands and feet of the swimmer, as they seek a 'fix' in water. If the hand stays in the same position for any period in time, then it will lose its 'purchase' and 'slip', for in that relative period the water will be moving in the direction of the pressure applied. But if the hand moves again to 'still' water then a new 'firm purchase' will be re-established and the body will be able once again to pole-vault and thrust forwards effectively.

Many people believe that a swimmer's arm action is contained in only one 'plane' (of a parallel order). However, in order to maintain an efficient 'catch' in water, the hand not only moves backwards but also outwards, inwards, upwards and downwards (relative to the sculling figure-of-eight synchro pattern). How does this occur? In, for example, the front crawl

Fig 6 *The angularly shaped blades of a propeller which normally turns in a clockwise direction. Because they are shaped they continually cut into 'still' water, and this ensures a firm purchase so pushing the ship forwards most effectively.*

stroke, the hands trace a shallow 'S' sculling path but this path is also complemented by longitudinal rolling movements of the body in the stroke; so the area of sculling pattern is increased inwardly, outwardly, upwards and downwards by natural movements of the body in the water. So although initially the depth at 'catch' is minimal, the hand will attain increasing depth due to the body roll.

The longitudinal roll in the opposite direction also assists the shallow outer 'scull' of arm; if the arm were to remain straight, it would travel upwards and out of the water. The arm, however, bends to the 'high elbow' position in order to preserve depth, then straightens in synchronized timing with the roll, which complements the exit phase of its action. During the backstroke arm cycle, the body roll also gives depth as the hand sinks to 'catch', so that a grown male competitive swimmer can attain a depth at 'catch' up to 45cm.

In breaststroke, the upper body starts to rise after 'catch' is attained in the water, and the hands have to travel downwards to maintain a 'fix' in the water. Because there is no longitudinal roll in this stroke, the outward scull is maintained by a wide arm action. As the body again sinks, the arms come from a high elbow position to an upward extension ahead.

In butterfly stroke, the hands sink to a deep catch as the body undulates on the downward cycle. As the rear end of the body sinks, the head starts to rise and the 'catch' is maintained by the high elbow position of the arms. As the arms go backwards, breathing inhalation is achieved by 'hyper extending' the head, this extension being necessary in order to maintain the body parallel to the surface of the water.

Up to two-thirds of the sculling pattern in butterfly stroke can be traced by following the pattern created by the air which is trapped by a swimmer's hands as they enter the water (see Fig 18). An experiment was attempted whereby the flow of air was increased so that the pattern could be observed to a greater degree. A bicycle inner tube was strapped round the body of a swimmer, and the air from it – the amount controlled by a valve

– made to flow down thin plastic tubes tied to the arms and leading down to the palms of the hands. The amount of air and the time it took to escape through the tubes into the hands was brief, but it was long enough for three or four camera exposures to be taken during various stroke cycles. The resulting transparencies and photographs (see Fig 18f) gave an in-depth awareness of stroke and sculling patterns, and particularly of the stroke patterns that associated the four strokes. Many coaches and teachers are still inclined to think that each stroke pattern and the mechanics of any one stroke are totally different from those of the other three. However, for those who believe in the principle of the wave form – 'S' pulling pattern – or 'sine' wave, then the arm and leg action of all strokes can be seen to be inter-related; this is shown clearly in Fig 7.

If it is feasible to agree on the inter-relationship of the front crawl, back crawl and butterfly, what association has the stroke patterns of breaststroke to the other three? From above, the complete cycle of the arm action may resemble a heart formation, but in fact the sculling action is also downwards and upwards. If

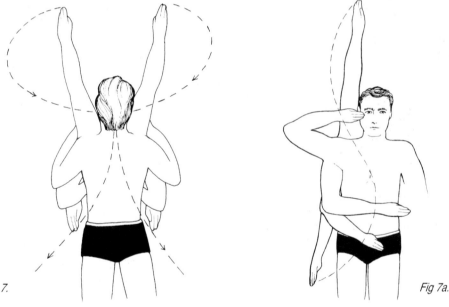

Fig 7.

Fig 7a.

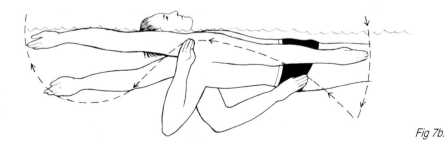

Fig 7b.

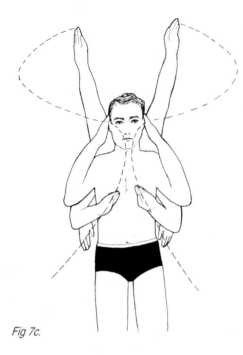

Fig 7c.

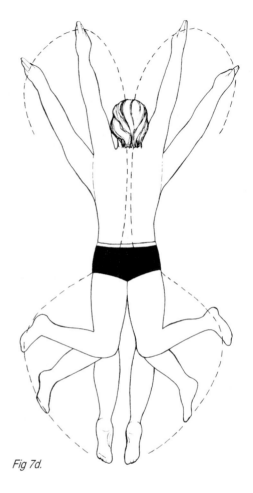

Fig 7d.

the stroke were swum with an alternating arm action, starting with the left arm, the path would resemble that of the front crawl, butterfly and perpendicular back crawl pattern.

Overall, the factor which should remain uppermost when teaching and coaching is that the body gains progression and momentum from the efficient 'fix' of a lever in water. And in order to maintain that 'fix', the lever must move constantly through a whole range of positions. In some respects it may be limited in its efficiency but the more talented swimmers can maintain and utilize it to a high degree of efficiency. A certain degree of 'slip' is of course inevitable with even the best of swimmers; many swimming teachers and coaches still extol the virtues of the 'push' and 'pull' in all strokes. But synchro swimmers are taught the principles of sculling at an early age, and the similarity between all four strokes and their sculling patterns is both remarkable and logical. These principles therefore far outweigh the theories which have been maintained in the past and which are now outmoded.

2

The Front Crawl Stroke

The fastest that a man can travel in water is approximately five miles an hour (8kph), and to attain this speed he would use the front crawl stroke because it is the fastest of the four competitive strokes. This is because a constant 'fix' is maintained on the water by the alternating actions of the arms and legs. There is no mention of front crawl as a stroke in the laws governing the sport. Thus the rules concerning this stroke come under the heading of freestyle, which is interpreted as any style other than backstroke, breaststroke or butterfly. In latter years the first stroke taught to beginners was breaststroke, but front crawl took over in popularity, one reason being the length of time taken to achieve efficient dorsiflexion of the feet.

The main difficulties generally experienced in the early stages of learning front crawl are these:

- Immersion of the face in the water.
- The action coming from the knee instead of the hip region.
- In the underwater phase, the arm tracing a straight path instead of a sculling one.
- The achievement of an efficient breathing cycle.

Once the above difficulties are improved upon, then a more streamlined body position – which is so important in any of the strokes – can be cultivated and acquired. Technique should be taught at an early age; usually this is at the 'improvement' stage once the swimmer has mastered the basics of the stroke in question. Every swimmer has individual characteristics in any of the four competitive strokes, and these idiosyncrasies will dictate a difference in both style and technique; the majority of swimmers have one or more factors that set them apart from others. Some are slimmer, some taller, others have different sized levers, but all are points which will lead to individual styles in the water. It is, however, worth noting that once swimmers have mastered the correctly taught techniques in starts and turns, the difference between individual styles in these aspects becomes negligible.

All the competitive strokes are performed in either the supine or the prone position but in neither one is it possible to exert the same amount of force that we can achieve in any position on terra firma. On land we often use our bodyweight to exert pressure on an object; in water, however, pressure is mainly achieved from the most appropriate lever. For example, the latissimus dorsi is the largest set of muscles in the upper body, and a longitudinal roll is instrumental in allowing these muscles to contribute to as long and as forceful a stroke as possible.

The front crawl has two main advantages as compared to the other three strokes. Firstly, the horizontal body position ensures efficient streamlining throughout the stroke cycle, therefore minimizing the resistance factors as described in Chapter 1.

Secondly, the alternating and continuous action of the arms and legs ensures that a high degree of mechanical force is exerted on the water. This results in a continuous, propulsive forward progression, as long as an efficient fix is established and maintained throughout the stroke cycle.

THE BODY POSITION

A good, efficient body position may be summarized thus:

The water level is at the forehead, with the body flat and streamlined but low enough in the water to give a good efficient kick. There are movements around the longitudinal axis as either hand sinks to 'catch', and the head is turned within its own axis for inhalation.

The position of the head in relation to the water level is always a good indication of body and streamlining efficiency. The longitudinal roll is so necessary in this stroke, for it not only assists progression but complements the sculling fix for 'still' water; it also places the body in a better position to create greater pressure, particularly in the latter phase of the arm action.

The body roll should be equal on both sides, so many coaches adopt the policy of teaching bilateral breathing because this will establish an equal balance in the stroke. It is also a useful way of 'sighting'

an opponent in a competition situation.

Excessive longitudinal movements lead only to stroke deficiencies; we see this in the early stages of learning, as the inexperienced swimmer over-rolls as he breathes. Extravagant head movements, too, are responsible for many problems in this and other strokes. Movements around the lateral axis (side to side) will also create deficiencies in the stroke; these lateral movements are usually brought about by:

1. 'Over-reaching', coupled with an entry over the centre line of the body.
2. A 'ballistic' arm recovery.
3. In the underwater phase, initial wide entry and 'pulling' too wide in the early part of the arm action.
4. Lateral movement of the head, usually in empathy with that of the arms as they enter over the centre line of the body.
5. 'Late breathing'(see Fig 17), when the head action stops momentarily, nestling into the shoulder. The arm recovery forwards causes the shoulder to come into contact with the head, moving it sharply back to the centre line. The head weighs approximately 10 per cent of the body-weight, so any sudden uncontrolled head movement is bound to create a reaction, in this case a sideways one. 'Late breathing' is a fault that many adult swimmers have. In the case of the unshaven male swimmer, the hard stubble on the chin leaves a red mark on the particular shoulder that the chin 'nestles' into during the breathing cycle.
6. On land, any sudden stopping of movement is absorbed by the ground we are standing on; in water the momentum is transferred to another part of the body – a factor which is used to good effect in both start and turn techniques. This principle is sometimes referred to as the 'transfer of momentum' or 'action and

Fig 8a   The very necessary longitudinal roll in the front crawl, shown in three different phases of the stroke.

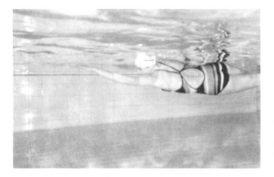

Fig 8b.

Fig 8c.

reaction'; so if an arm, for example, is suddenly stopped in its movement on entering the water after a ballistic type of recovery, then a lateral leg movement will occur in the opposite direction.

We know that the leg action helps to

balance the particular fault and stabilize the body position. In order specifically to target and emphasize the reason for the lateral movement, it is sometimes helpful to nullify the leg action completely by using a pull buoy, or tube around the feet. Both the teacher and coach will sometimes have to employ corrective practices and coaching points in order to eradicate problems, and this must be done early on, before the faults become ingrained into the style of the individual swimmers concerned.

THE LEG ACTION

A good, efficient leg action may be summarized thus:

The leg action comes from the hip region, and passes down through the knee which bends due to the pressure of water and to the timing of the levers for the propulsive phase in the kick down. It finishes at the feet, which are plantar-flexed and whip-like in their action. The leg action is continuous and alternating, with the feet working close together.

The leg action in the front crawl accomplishes several necessary functions:

1.   It gives supplementary propulsion, even with a highly efficient arm action (that is, when one arm enters as the other arm leaves the water). If any degree of 'catch-up' is introduced into the arm action, the legs are made to work progressively harder. As the amount of 'catch-up' increases, it has an inhibiting effect on forward progression, though how much relates to the proportion of 'catch-up' in the arm action.

2.   The *total* area of the leg bearing down on the water keeps the body high and

maintains the body in an efficient, streamlined position. However, if the leg action is initiated from the knee, the knee will 'vee' down in the water and this will result in some degree of positional incline and a subsequent increase in profile resistance (see Fig 5).

3.   When the arm enters the water, the opposite leg kicks in a downward direction. Due to the body roll, the directional force of this is oblique (angular).

4.   The leg action also counteracts excessive lateral and longitudinal movements of the body. These originate from lack of co-ordination and imperfect technique in the arm and head action.

There are many different styles of kick to be seen in the front crawl, but although individuals may interpret the technique in different ways, this has no bearing on the 'pattern' of kick. Basically there are three different, even kicking patterns; from these three, some others also emerge or rather diverge. The three are:

1.   The straight two-beat kick; this can lead to the two-beat crossover kick.

2.   The straight four-beat kick; this can lead to the one-two-three crossover kick.

3.   The straight six-beat kick.

Various theories exist concerning the drag effect of the legs and feet. For example there is a definite drag effect if the feet are not efficiently plantar-flexed. Also, in the two-beat kicking cycle the feet of some swimmers hardly move and this immediately gives rise to the drag theory. However, this particular action of the legs and feet reminds me of water flowing along the hull of the ship and meeting a slightly inclined rudder, and this rudder is helping to keep the ship on course. In the same way the foot in a downward movement traces out an angular path, and the water flowing along the body and then

away from the angular area of the foot appears to be having a stabilizing influence. This theory seems far more logical to comprehend. The female swimmer is far more buoyant than the average male, and for this reason the amount of 'bearing area' leg kicks can be kept to a minimum. Many swimmers in a training programme adopt a two-beat kicking pattern; but when the same swimmers are speeded up, the pattern can change to a six-beat one.

The straight 'two-beat' kick: the opposite leg kicks downwards as the hand sinks to 'catch'; thus as the right hand sinks to 'catch', the left leg kicks downwards and vice versa. This is the easiest action to comprehend in front crawl stroke analysis. The more difficult sequence to analyse is the **'two-beat crossover'** action. From a 'crossover' position where the right foot is above the left foot, the knee bends on the right leg, bringing it up to the surface, from where it kicks down in an angular path (due to body roll and lateral movement). It then comes upwards to 'tuck in' under the left foot, again assuming a 'crossover' position. During this action the left leg has moved slightly downwards, outwards and back inwards; it traces a semi-circular path before completing the 'crossover' position above the right foot. There is a momentary pause before commencement of the next cycle, when the left knee now bends, taking the lower leg up to the surface for the kick downwards.

The objective of the whole kicking cycle is undoubtedly to stabilize the body position, the propulsive factor being so slight as to be almost negligible. At the 'crossover' position the feet are plantar-flexed and adopt a 'pencil'-like shape, so that water flows through and away. The amount of viscous drag is completely minimized with this action.

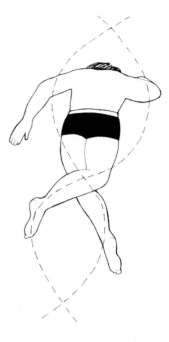

Fig 9   The two-beat kicking cycle.

The major kick downwards has a bearing factor on the water for body streamlining, although lateral deviations may still occur, even with a high elbow recovery. In the two-beat kick, some lateral deviation is created by the 'assistance' of a sideways movement from the trunk of the body; this sideways deviation is controlled by the 'crossover' action in the kicking cycle. There are, however, *four* distinct movements in the leg action: as one foot travels up to the surface, the other moves downwards, around, and then finishes above the other foot, after that foot accelerates down and back up. The top foot now moves up to the surface and accelerates downwards. Thus it can be argued that the 'two-beat crossover' kick is indeed one of a four-beat pattern.

The four-beat pattern: In order to simulate the so-called 'two'-beat crossover action, place one hand on top of the other, move the top hand beneath the lower and repeat, using an up-and-down movement

for both hands – and so you have the whole two-beat kicking cycle as in Fig 9. However, the movement of the foot travelling down is designated as the numerical factor in any kicking pattern so there are in fact four movements of the feet in this cycle; two are positive downward movements, and two are involuntary or 'placement' movements. The same could be said for the four-beat pattern, except that the 'placement movements' have a more positive downbeat; moreover in many cases this pattern will revert to that of the 'crossover' format in one phase of the leg cycle.

The crossover pattern will counteract any lateral deviation created by excessive movement of the head in the breathing cycle; the complete kicking cycle as described above will now result in a one-two-three crossover pattern. The 'four-beat' action also has a mainly stabilizing influence; it has only a limited propulsive factor.

The six-beat leg pattern: In front crawl this is difficult to assess in exact relation to the arm cycle, although limiting the speed of the movement allows a comprehensive evaluation of what is happening:

1. As the right arm sinks to catch, the left leg kicks downwards.
2. As the right arm nears completion of the inward scull, the right leg kicks downwards.
3. As the right arm is at exit, the left leg kicks downwards.
4. As the left arm sinks to catch, the right leg kicks downwards.
5. As the left arm nears completion of the inward scull, the left leg kicks downwards.
6. As the left arm is at exit, the right leg kicks down.

The six-beat leg action assists the arm action by giving a good level of supplementary propulsion; it also maintains a streamlined body position. It is used mainly in sprint events, although this is not to say that it is never used by the distance swimmer. The same could be said of the 'two-beat' and the 'two-beat crossover' kicking patterns, both of which have been successfully employed by club swimmers and by swimmers of international calibre in sprint events.

The Importance of Timing

Certain swimmers find difficulty while engaged in kicking drills; the subject is usually dismissed with a shrug of the shoulders and a reference to the swimmer being a poor kicker. This situation can be redressed, however, by examining the leg as three separate levers: the upper leg, the lower leg and the foot. Timing is of critical importance in the inter-reaction of each limb movement, and the flexibility of the foot is of vital importance; if the angle and timing between any of the levers is wrong, then the leg action becomes inefficient. (See also the section on Timing and Co-ordination, p. 30.) The kick comes from the hip region, acts down through the knee which bends in the kick down, and finishes at the foot, which moves in a downward and upward direction. Each lever covers its own separate range in movement. An efficient kicking action should trace out a wave-like pattern (Fig 10).

The Importance of the Foot

The most important of the three levers in relation to propulsion is the foot: if there is a lack of flexibility here, then the amount of propulsion is severely affected. Some breaststrokers find it hard to attain an efficient plantar flexion of the feet, and this compromises the propulsive element of their front crawl. But whichever pattern a swimmer has adopted for the stroke, that pattern cannot be changed by the coach – although the style, or the

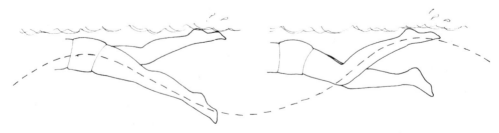

Fig 10   Leg action and kicking pattern.

swimmer's understanding of the leg action can sometimes be improved by the observant teacher. This is done by compiling knowledge of the leg action, and by logical progressive practices in the areas of timing and flexibility.

THE ARM ACTION

A good, efficient arm action may be summarized thus:

From the 'catch' position, the hands flex slightly then scull outwards, backwards, downwards and then inwards, tracing a slightly outward path back to the end of the costume; the elbow then exits the water first, followed by the little finger. The whole sculling pattern is in the form of a shallow 'S'. Recovery of the arm is with the elbow in a high position and the entry of the hand into the water takes place approximately 45cm in front of and in line with the shoulder. After entry, the hand extends ahead before sinking to 'catch'.

The 'Catch' stage

The 'catch' stage takes place approximately 15 to 20cm under the water, after the arm reaches full extension; the hand (with a movement controlled by the flexors) angles slightly and achieves a 'catch' on the water (this flexing movement should, at this stage of the arm action, be relative to the other three strokes). The elbow should not be higher than the hand during this stage; the arm should be in the form of a straight lever at 'catch'; if there is still flexion in the arm at this stage the outcome is undesirable depth leading to a deep 'catch' and a curtailed sculling pattern.

The 'catch' is the first action of the

hand in the water, and it has a stabilizing influence. The rest of the underwater phase in the arm action will be referred to as a 'fix' and is the propulsive phase. The 'catch'/'fix' on the water should be maintained as efficiently as possible throughout the entire underwater arm action, although having said that, even the best of swimmers have difficulty in achieving a perfect 'fix' throughout this phase. As already explained if the hand stays too long in one position, it will 'slip' because the water is moving in that relative period of time.

Fig 11 The 'catch' position.

The Propulsive Phase

The hand now travels outwards and backwards, downwards and inwards, and the 'fix is effectively maintained by finding 'still' water in the sculling area. The entire sculling action is carried out by co-ordinated movements of the upper and lower arms and the hand acting as three levers.

So, having established 'catch', the arm moves outwards (Fig 12), then inwards, with the elbow assuming an increasing angle until it reaches a maximum degree of bend at the completion of the inward scull. This angle between upper and lower arm should realize about 90 degrees, although it was seen to vary

Fig 12   *Outward scull in front crawl.*

Fig 14a   *The arm exiting the water with the little finger leading the hand recovery.*

Fig 13   *The half-diamond position of the arm completing the inward scull.*

Fig 14b   *The 'high elbow' recovery.*

between individual swimmers. A half-diamond position (as shown in Fig 13) is the most efficient one to have at the completion of the inward scull. From this position, the hand traces a movement outwards and back to the end of the costume. The elbow is seen to break the surface of the water first, followed by the little finger of the hand (Fig 14a). In an extended position ahead of the swimmer, the arm is relatively weak; however, the degree of power increases during the inward sculling phase and reaches maximum proportions during the backward phase. With an efficient 'fix' the talented swimmer can reach these maximum proportions. The stroke of the less able swimmer, however, cannot attain the same levels of power and efficiency because of the amount his hand will 'slip' in his stroke cycle.

In this phase, the longitudinal roll is not only vital to progression, it also facilitates extension ahead, depth in the underwater phase and recovery of the hand and arm.

The Recovery Phase

There are different types of recovery for the arms, and which one the individual swimmer adopts gives a good idea as to his ability. The most efficient is the 'high elbow' recovery: there are no lateral movements and the hand can be placed perfectly for entry, either in line with the ear or within the width of the shoulders.

A 'throwing' movement, or a straight arm recovery over the water, will lead to a degree of lateral movement in the body; in many cases the hand will enter across the central body line, and this makes it difficult to place it correctly before sliding to 'catch'. Without an efficient 'catch' there are bound to be corresponding problems for the initial propulsive phase. It is a fault which should be redressed in a swimmer's early stages of improvement, or catered for with technique drills in the normal schedule practices.

The Entry Phase

The entry phase of the hand is so closely related to arm recovery that it is important to associate the two actions in a compatible manner: thus an efficient arm recovery dictates the level of efficiency in the arm entry; equally, inefficiency in the recovery promotes an inefficient entry. The following variations can be seen in the entry position:

1. 'Soft' hand entry.
2. 'Hard' hand entry.
3. 'Straight' arm entry.
4. 'Catch-up.'

If the hand is placed in line correctly entry can either be 'soft' or 'hard'. In a **'soft'**, entry the thumb will enter first with the hand at an angle of approximately 30 degrees; this ensures little entrapment of air in the passage down to the 'catch' position.

In a **'hard'** entry, the flat of the hand will entrap air, which will continue to flow upwards from the palm; some coaches consider this reduces the amount of 'feel' on the initial 'catch'. Whichever method of entry is used, the hand now extends ahead to the full length of the arm, then drops at an angle before once again attaining the 'catch' position.

There is also the **'straight arm'** recovery, where the arm is extended ahead over the water as one lever and then brought down to 'catch'.

'**Catch-up**' can vary as to the degree with which one hand catches up the other in the arm cycle. One hand goes through its arm cycle and then unites with the other arm, either in extension ahead or in the 'catch' position. 'Catch-up' is also used as a drill to ensure good extension in the arm action. It does, however, create an 'overload' on the leg action; because the arm cycle is not continuous, the legs have to work harder.

Front Crawl Sequence

Fig 15a The entry is either 'hard' or 'soft', with the hand sliding forwards just under the surface of the water before dropping to catch. The opposite leg (the right in this picture) kicks down with the foot 'toed in', so achieving a greater bearing on the surface of the water.

Fig 15b The arm is fully extended, the body streamlined; the head is perfectly placed, the water surface level with the forehead.

Fig 15c   Having accomplished an efficient catch, the hand has flexed, 'fixed' onto the water and is starting its outward sweep.

Fig 15f   The arm pushes backwards for the final phase; this part of the stroke holds the greatest velocity. The hand is efficiently placed, palm facing directly backwards.

Fig 15g   Having accomplished its contribution to forward velocity, the hand now turns palm inwards for exit and recovery from the water.

Fig 15d   The elbow starts to bend, bringing the hand inwards.

BREATHING

A good, efficient breathing action may be summarized thus:

Breathing is unilateral or bilateral. The swimmer inhales (in a trough) near the end of the push phase; trickle or explosive exhalation takes place throughout the remainder of the arm cycle.

Fig 15e   The hand continues to come in on the inward sweep until the angle of 90 degrees is completed. The path of the hand (the pulling pattern) is shown clearly by the trailing pattern of air.

On land we take breathing for granted; in water, however, breathing must be synchronized to the stroke cycle. When allied to the stroke and timing of a proficient swimmer, there should only be minor problems to contend with; but at improver level the breathing action is a recurring problem both for the teacher and coach. So often the main emphasis is placed on inhalation, although the greater part of the stroke cycle is spent exhaling; when breathing is taught, the emphasis should focus on exhalation as it relates to the timing factor of the whole action.

In training sessions and some public swimming, the following breathing techniques are seen:

- Unilateral breathing/over-rolling to breathe
- Bilateral breathing
- Late breathing
- Explosive breathing
- Breath holding
- Controlled or hypoxic breathing

When the head turns so as to take in air, the longitudinal movement of the body is increased by another 20 or 30 degrees. The breathing cycle therefore affects the body position and so also its streamlining.

Breathing in the Trough

The forward motion of the swimmer's body creates a bow wave and its accompanying trough; the swimmer can turn

Fig 16 Breathing in the 'trough' in front crawl.

his head at each arm cycle and inhale in this trough, when it appears that inhalation is taking place beneath the general water line (Fig 16). As the swimmer becomes more proficient the speed through the water increases, with a corresponding increase in the size of bow wave. The trough also increases in size, so that minimal head movement is required in order to take in oxygen.

An efficient breathing action occurs when the head movement is synchronized to that of the arm action. The head should start to turn when the arm in the water is early in the propulsive phase; the head movement is completed as the hand is at exit and then follows the hand through to entry. The breathing action continues throughout the full arm cycle. A descriptive phrase such as 'explosive breathing' refers mainly to inhalation.

Breathing Techniques

Unilateral breathing can lead to a 'loping' type of movement which will affect the stroke balance; improver swimmers should therefore be taught the fundamentals of bilateral breathing techniques at an early age.

Bilateral breathing improves balance, and in a competition situation allows the monitoring of swimmers in adjacent lanes.

'Late breathing' is a fault that exists not only among social swimmers, but also in more competent swimmers. It involves a momentary restriction in the head movement after inhalation has taken place, when the shoulder of the recovering arm meets up with the head which now turns to the front 'late' in the arm action (Fig 17). Although this is a common fault among competitive swimmers, there has been some success in overcoming it. The coaching point should be to 'follow the thumb' throughout the arm cycle; moreover if the thumb has a bright piece of tape wrapped around it, is much easier to see and the head may now synchronize with this target.

Fig 17   Late breathing in front crawl. The swimmer's head stays within the shoulder region as the arm continues forwards to the entry position.

'**Breath holding**' should be widely used in a competitive situation; it is especially important in the race plan when deciding the number of strokes that should be completed at the start, turn and finish before a breath is taken.

In the early stages of a beginner's education 'breath holding' is taught in situations where the teacher wishes to implement a better body position and streamlining. The non-breathing situation can also be used to perfect a selected technique in the stroke. A specific or limited breathing cycle would be the next progressive step.

TIMING AND CO-ORDINATION

An efficiently co-ordinated action may be summarized thus:

There are two, four or six beats of the legs to one complete arm cycle, with continuity of arm and leg movements.

Good co-ordination, or timing, refers to the number of kicks or leg actions to one complete arm cycle. In stroke analysis, mistakes are made in synchronizing the arm cycle and breathing routine to the leg action. When co-ordinating the front crawl, the swimmer kicks in even multiples: as one hand enters the water and sinks to 'catch', then that same hand re-enters after one complete stroke cycle is finished. The even multiples in this stroke are described in depth under the section 'Leg action', as are the different kicking patterns associated with this stroke

THE TEACHING AND EARLY COACHING OF FRONT CRAWL STROKE

After attaining a reasonable body position, stroke technique can be improved with progressive teaching practices. In general there is always a tendency for speed, but this should be curbed. Teach this stroke in sectional parts, each with a relevant exercise, then the whole stroke.

Inefficient leg action can be responsible for an inclined body position and lateral deviation. Look for the head being buried in the water; this may raise the hips, but the remedy could be exercises to improve the leg action.

A proficient breaststroker may have difficulty in achieving good plantarflexion while swimming either front or back crawl. In the downward action of the front crawl, the knees bend due to the pressure of water and the timing of the levers in the kicking action. This action occurs naturally, but if emphasized when teaching the stroke, it will lead to the kick coming from the knees and not the hips. Make swimmers conscious of the leg action: make them swim full stroke, and think half-way about the arm action, then the leg action.

Avoid giving several teaching points at a time, especially concerning the arm action. Concentrate on one at a time, with a technically descriptive demonstration.

	Drills	*Purpose*	*Teaching Points*
Front Crawl Body Position			
1.	Breath hold; push and glide then 2/4/6 kicks	Introductory	Hips up; shoulders square; as speed drops start the kick sequence
2.	Holding float: 4/6/8 kicks, then breathe	Introductory	Eyes target under the float
3.	Arms extended: 4/6/8 kicks, then breathe	Introductory	Look over extended hands
4.	Swim 1 width, or 1 length	Introductory	Breathe every 4/6 strokes; look over the extended hand on entry
5.	Push off; glide; swim 4/6 strokes; swim 1 width or 1 length	Introductory	Streamlined body; water level to the forehead
6.	Swim 1 width or 1 length	Improver stage	Breathe every 4/6 strokes; look over the extended hand on entry
Front Crawl Leg Action			
1.	With float; head up	General drill	Plantar-flex feet; kick from hips not knees; point toes; legs pass closely together
2.	With float; target time	Overload drill	Kick on target time 5 × 100 on 2.30, target time 1.30/1.40.
3.	With angled float	Increased resistance	
4.	Arms crossed locked ahead	Increased resistance	Keep streamlined position
5.	Arms crossed behind body	Resistance or hypoxic drill	Normal breathing, or breathe every 20 kicks
6.	Kicking in waves 2 × width/lengths	Overload drill	Boys at one end, girls at the other; if caught, lose a life (× 3)

	Drills	Purpose	Teaching Points
7.	One arm extended ahead; other at the side	Achieves body roll	6/8/10 kicks, then alternate arms
8.	Kick easy length, then increase kicking cycles	Overload drill	Alternate length 10/20 secs faster
9.	Any of the above with flippers	Ankle flexibility	
10.	Catch-up crawl; alternate 2/4/6 any multiples	Overloads leg action/improves arm extensions	Hand recovers to hand, then extends ahead for catch
11.	Catch-up crawl, then kicking multiples	Mainly improves leg action	
12.	Kicking multiples then stroke multiples	Stroke transfer	
13.	Kick a 'locomotive' set	Sustained overload	1 easy, 1 hard/2 easy, 2 hard up to 4/6 and down

Front Crawl Arm Action

1.	Standing: on side or in water	Introductory	Finger-tip sliding entry in line with shoulder; hand slides to catch; hand flexes with elbow raised in pull phase, scull under body; thumb to costume; high elbow recovery
2.	Walk crawl into over balance	Introductory	
3.	Arms only: pull buoy	Concentration on arm arm action; high elbow	Thumb to costume; thumb to armpit; thumb to side of head and enter
4.	Feet crossed: pull buoy	Resistance	
5.	Feet in inner tube	Resistance	Can add a target time
6.	'Spearing fish' achieves a shallower 'catch'	Improves extension	Extend into the roll
7.	Alternating or single arm catch-up	Promotes in-line entry, reach	Sliding hand entry; angular hand at catch
8.	Fist drill arm action	Promotes high elbow	Create an 'S' sculling pattern; use the elbow as the paddle

	Drills	Purpose	Teaching Points
9.	Use of hand paddles	Works muscle groups	
10.	Count strokes widths/ lengths	Longer stroke	Return 2 strokes less; fingers closed

Front Crawl Breathing Action

1.	Breathing action on pool side; stationary drill; then in water	Awareness of breathing techniques	Head turns, not body; inhale as head turns; blow out as head returns to centre line
2.	In water holding on to rail; gentle kick	Introductory	Head just clears water, blow out underwater; head rolls like a ball, so that one eye and half mouth clears the water
3.	Breathing with kicking action; short distances, hand-held float	Improver stage	Control over turning the head
4.	Alternate arm action, hand-held float, short distance	Improver stage	'Follow the thumb' throughout (can improve 'late breathing')
5.	Push and glide, then one breathing cycle/arm cycle	Improver stage	No breath holding
6.	Bilateral breathing cycle on pool side then in water	Creates smoother, balanced stroke	Breathe every three pulls; alternate head turning
7.	Controlled breathing and hypoxic drills	Can assist 'race plan'	Don't breathe into stroke/ finish, or out of the turn
8.	'Follow the thumb' drill	'Late' breathing drill	Tie a bright piece of plastic on the thumb; head will then follow the arm movement cycle through to hip

Front Crawl Timing

The timing in front crawl is natural and differs with each individual swimmer. In training a sprinter may train 'two-beat' then change to a 'six-beat kick' as the tempo of training increases.

3

The Butterfly Stroke

Before the butterfly stroke was accepted, there were only three other strokes: breaststroke, backstroke and freestyle. Then just before World War II, a number of breaststrokers adopted an innovative style in which they pushed backwards, then brought both arms out and over the water in the recovery phase. After World War II, most of the top swimmers could manage a whole race using this butterfly/breaststroke technique. In 1947 Roy Romain won the European 200 metres breaststroke using the butterfly arm action with breaststroke leg action and from then on, no breaststrokers won any races with conventional breaststroke arm action. As a result of this, breaststroke and butterfly were separated, and the dolphin leg movement became synonymous with the butterfly arm action.

Jack Hale won the first 200-metre butterfly championship using a deep continual kicking routine, followed by a slow arm movement. This style involved a great oxygen debt and a powerful leg action, and was followed by all until 1956 when the Hungarian Gregor Tumpeck won convincingly at Blackpool with a two-beat dolphin leg action with a continuous arm action. This technique became known as 'sliding butterfly'. Following this, Bill Yorzick (USA) won the Olympic gold medal using Tumpeck's technique, and subsequently the rest of the world also adopted it. This is the butterfly stroke as we now know it.

GENERAL TECHNIQUE

In certain quarters butterfly is considered with a degree of trepidation by teachers, coaches and swimmers alike. In fact it would be more accurate to refer to it as 'dolphin stroke', for undulation is of paramount importance in achieving success; as mentioned above, the stroke was called 'butterfly' because of the transformed arm action, recovery taking place over the water instead of under it. Emphasis has always been on the recovery phase rather than the underwater phase of the stroke; this emphasis still exists and it can be detrimental because many will concentrate on this part of the cycle before vital basics are mastered. The arm action in butterfly consists of a breaststroke outward and inward 'scull' with a double arm, front crawl forward phase. It is in this latter phase that difficulties are encountered, usually not only due to lack of strength but also because the swimmer still lacks the necessary coordination in his basic techniques.

Another important consideration is this: the downward and upward movement of the the legs in butterfly comes from the hip region. Teachers and coaches must bear in mind that if emphasis is placed on the leg action as a 'kicking action' instead of 'hip movement', then the movement will tend to come from the knee and this has severe consequences for any swimmer in any learning situation. In those circumstances when it is unavoidable to use the expression 'kicking action', it should be done so sparingly and with care.

THE BODY POSITION

An efficient body position may be summarized thus:

The body position throughout the stroke cycle is synchronized with the arm and leg movements, and undulating. The position of the hips midway through the cycle of undulation dictates the degree to which the body is streamlined. The mid-portion of the swimmer is above the general water level in the leg movement down; then during the push and recovery phase, the hips fall to a level just under the surface of the water. The head, arm and leg actions must be continuous, with the arm and leg actions simultaneous throughout.

The body position changes constantly throughout the complete stroke cycle. However, during the principal propulsive phase the body should be in a streamlined position, and how successfully it achieves this is dictated by the hip position; the hip position also indicates the efficiency of undulation. As specified above, in order for efficient undulation to take place, the head, arm and leg actions must be continuous with the movements of the arms and legs precisely synchronized. Undulation is the prime considera-

tion in this stroke, and the major factors responsible for its successful achievement are these:

1. Head movement: chin to chest.
2. The arm action, primarily on entry and into the 'catch' position.
3. The leg action, which if generated from the hip region, causes the hips to rise. It also contributes to propulsion.

The degree to which the body undulates downwards as well as upwards needs to be controlled efficiently. In order to achieve the necessary depth in the downward movement, the swimmer has to make full use of his levers: thus the upper body rises as the back end starts to fall, and the head comes from the chin-to-chest position and hyper-extends in preparation for oxygen inhalation. This head movement significantly affects the degree to which the body inclines; if it is excessive, then the body position is adversely effected. The movement upwards should therefore be limited and controlled, in contrast to the more substantial movement required in the downward direction (chin-to-chest).

Without propulsive force and progression forwards, the inclined downward angle of the body would assume significant proportions. However, the level of forward velocity counteracts the level of tilt in the body, and establishes a level plane of undulation; thus in competition, speed and velocity are the major considerations and accordingly the pattern of the leg action changes from 'major/minor' to 'minor/major'.

The factors which create undulation contribute equally to a symmetry of movement that makes the dolphin stroke idyllic in its flowing motion. However, in order to appreciate fully the extent to which undulation is created by the head movement, ask the swimmer to swim 'chin-on-the-water butterfly'; it will be seen that this drastically affects the flowing motion of undulation. Try this over half a length, then re-introduce the head action.

THE LEG ACTION

An efficient leg action may be summarized thus:

From a depth of about two feet (half a metre) and in a movement generated from the hip region, the legs start to rise upwards. The upper leg then starts to fall, while the lower leg continues to the surface. Next, the lower leg accelerates downwards until it comes back in line with the upper leg. This downward movement of the legs assists propulsion; and in its execution the hips are raised, which re-establishes the streamlined body position. The leg action is simultaneous and continuous throughout. The feet are pointed with an angular movement, ensuring that the maximum surface area is brought to bear on the water in both up and down phases of the leg action.

As specified above, the butterfly leg action has two functions: it assists propulsion, but more importantly it raises the hips mid-way through undulation and thereby maintains the body position. There are no lateral or longitudinal movements because of the simultaneous arm action. The leg action is exceptionally simple to define in terms of timing, unlike the kicking multiples in front crawl. Thus one undulation begins as the hands drop to 'catch', the other as they near the exit phase and so in terms of good competitive efficiency the stroke has a two-beat kicking action. Examples of less efficient styles in leg action include:

- The breaststroke leg action.
- The one-beat pattern.
- Kicking from the knee.
- The two-beat 'slow tempo' cycle.

The breaststroke leg action establishes a fix on the water and helps in forward progression. However, it contributes almost nothing to the undulation factor in the stroke. The necessary undulation and the streamlining of the body is therefore accomplished by the arms and head having to work harder.

The one-beat pattern is used mainly by improver swimmers, although some competitive swimmers may 'hang on' at the end of a hard race because they haven't the energy left to continue the two-beat rhythm. However, this leads to the loss of streamlining and propulsion, and to an inclined body position.

Kicking from the knee achieves the bare minimum of propulsion in the stroke; the body position is inclined, and these swimmers will probably do their level best never to swim or train on butterfly. So, they must be brought back to early practices, building the movement up slowly with the hands at the side, and over short distances (see the penultimate section to this chapter 'Teaching and Early Coaching of the Butterfly Stroke').

THE ARM ACTION

An efficient arm action may be summarized thus:

The thumbs enter the water in line with the shoulders and drop to a deep catch. Initially the hands scull in a sideways/ upwards and outward path, mainly due to the undulating movement of the body;

they continue to travel outwards, downwards and inwards. The elbows are now higher than the hands and on the inward sculling path the fingers almost touch. From this point the hands travel outwards and backwards to the hips; they then turn palm inwards. The arm exits from the water with the elbow leading, followed by the little finger. The recovery of the arms over the water is ballistic, with the arms stretched and straight.

The 'Catch'

The 'catch' in butterfly is deep, depending on the size of the individual swimmer's levers; for the average competitive swimmer it is certainly deeper than 30cm. As well as the arms 'knifing' downwards, the body is also at its deepest point of undulation and these two contributory factors explain the depth of the hands at this point. Once the necessary depth has been reached the hands flex and 'fix' onto the water.

The Propulsive Phase

The three levers which are so necessary for undulation are synchronized in timing and continuity of movement. As soon as the body attains its maximum depth in frontal undulation, it then starts to move upwards. The hands now move outwards, upwards, downwards and then inwards, the elbows bending and attaining a high position; the hands almost touch before pressing outwards and backwards. Throughout the whole underwater phase of the arm action, the hand angles are continually changing; during the backward underwater phase, the angle changes so the hand is at approximately 90 degrees to the lower arm, with the full area of the palm facing backwards. The elbow breaks the surface of the water first, followed by the little finger of each hand.

When swum efficiently, one complete arm cycle will give forward progression of one complete body-length.

Just as in the other three competitive strokes, the power of the stroke increases during the inward sculling phase and reaches maximum velocity in the final backward phase; at this stage the simultaneous and double arm action has a greater power ratio than any other stroke. It is during the recovery stage that forward progression slacks off, however, and as regards being the fastest of the competitive strokes, butterfly takes second place behind front crawl with its continuous and alternating action.

Because of the difference in levels of strength, a female swimmer will have a smaller area of 'scull' in the outward and inward sculling phase. Moreover if the elbows are dropped and allowed to come into the ribs, then the amount of power that is exerted on the water by the arms is proportionally reduced.

The Recovery Phase

The recovery phase of the arms is accomplished by two factors:

- The muscle groups responsible for the recovery movement.
- A forward movement of the body instigated by the downward action of the legs.

The arms recover in an extended position, passing as close as is possible over the water surface; the hands are inclined with the thumbs turning downwards. If the arms were to recover one at a time in turn, lateral movement would be created; the fact that they recover together makes any lateral movement impossible.

The Entry Phase

There are three variations that can occur in the 'entry' phase:

1. 'Soft' or 'hard' entry.
2. Little finger leading.
3. Entry wide of the shoulder line.

The entry in line with the shoulders can be either 'soft' or 'hard' before the hands slip forwards and down to the 'catch' position. If 'hard', when the palm of the hands is presented to the water, the amount of depth is fractionally less and this could proportionally affect undulation, particularly as the hands must now turn palm outwards to find a proficient 'catch' and then 'fix' on the water. If this action is fractionally delayed, it will lead to the 'catch' in its early stages being inefficient. In a 'soft' entry the hands enter and then slide forwards and down with no delay – and if entry is accomplished with the thumbs leading, there is minimal resistance down to the initial 'catch' position. The contribution to undulation is therefore maximized, and because the palms already face outwards, the initial stage of the arm action is accomplished with optimal effect.

Butterfly Stroke Sequence

Fig 18a   In the butterfly arm action the hands enter ahead and in line with the shoulders. In a training situation and in some competitive situations, the major kick now occurs as the hands enter and drop to 'catch'.

Fig 18b   After entry the hands drop to catch. This is a 'hard' entry, with the palms of the hands being presented to the water.

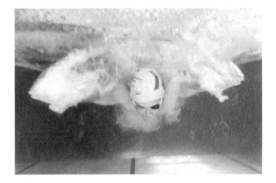

Fig 18c   The hands start to flex as the arms also begin to flex at the elbows. In order to highlight the propulsive pattern of the arm action, air was introduced in the palms of the hands. This shows clearly the outward, downward and inward sculling patterns of the hands as they achieve a continual 'fix' on the water with an elaborate range of movements.

Fig 18d   The elbows continue to bend so the hands can forge a deeper path.

Fig 18e   The arms are now in the 'high elbow' position; the hands move continually throughout the complete stroke cycle, and at this point are starting to 'come around the bend', turning to face inwards for the inner sweep.

Fig 18h   Air is taken in after the mouth has cleared the water; the head is hyper-extended to help breathing, and also to improve streamlining in the body position.

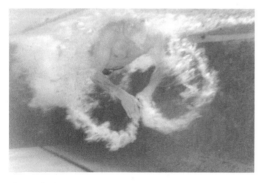

Fig 18f   The arms continue to bend at the elbows, so the hands continue to find 'still' water as they move upwards. The pattern of air shows the complete sphere of arm movement throughout this phase of the arm action.

Fig 18i   When inhalation is complete, the head moves downwards. Both arms have exited from the water and are in the primary recovery stage.

Fig 18g   The arms continue to press back to the end of the costume, then the palms turn inwards towards the hip. The recovery is with the elbow followed by the little finger.

Fig 18j   The ballistic movement close to and over the water; it is very important that the head enters the water ahead of the hands.

BREATHING

An efficient breathing technique may be summarized thus:

As the arms are pushing backwards to the hips, the head breaks the surface of the water, then hyper-extends to take in oxygen. At this 'intake' stage, the arms are exiting the water in the first phase of recovery. Exhalation is accomplished throughout the rest of the stroke cycle. The breathing action takes place during every second stroke cycle.

As detailed above, inhalation takes place in accordance with the arm action. The head movement is continuous throughout the stroke cycle, and this is necessary both for the breathing cycle and for its contribution to undulation. There are many and varied breathing patterns, most referring to the number of times inhalation takes place:

1. Breathing one and one (every stroke)
2. Breathing one and two – one and three
3. Breathing two and two
4. Breathing two and three
5. Side-breathing

Raising the head to take in oxygen nearly always affects body streamlining, and the less infrequently it is raised, the better profile resistance will be. The age group swimmer must be made aware of the need to establish an individual breathing pattern; this should be determined in training routines and then implemented in the overall race plan.

'Side-breathing' appears to be an individual preference; swimmers who do this do it naturally, and many have difficulty in changing the pattern. The action gives the impression that the head is not raised as high as the more conventional method of breathing. In the front crawl stroke, breathing to the side is obligatory, but the swimmer is assisted in this action by the longitudinal rolling movement. Because the movement in butterfly is undulating, the swimmer gets no assistance in the turning of the head; it requires particular effort, although he or she would deny this. Let him try conventional practices, however, and gauge the results accordingly. Nevertheless it is an individual preference: if the swimmer's times are satisfactory, then this practice must be accepted as a matter of personal choice.

Fig 19   Breathing to the side in butterfly stroke.

TIMING AND CO-ORDINATION

Efficient co-ordination may be summarized thus:

There is a two-beat leg action to one complete arm cycle: the downbeat of the larger kick takes place as the hands are at 'catch', and the smaller kick takes place as the hands are near the end of the push-through.

Although the leg action is continuous throughout the arm cycle (occurring twice), it is far easier to estimate when the downbeats occur by the position of the arms. Thus the first downbeat is completed as the hands are in the 'catch' position; the second occurs near the end of the push-through.

In training we refer to the leg action as being 'major/minor'. In competition and if the swimmer is at sprint speed, then the leg action sequence changes to 'minor/major'. There are various explanations for this occurrence, and one of the more logical ones concerns both the body position and the propulsion factor. In the body position, three factors combine to cause the hips to fall:

1. The initial phase of the arm recovery, when the head is raised for inhalation.
2. The recovery of the arms over the water.
3. The upward movement of the legs (after the downbeat movement).

The body at this phase of the stroke is at its lowest position of incline (although it is interesting to note that the amount the hips fall with a swimmer of good technique is approximately a mere 10–15cm in total). The powerful downbeat of the legs complements the stroke as follows:

- At this point the arm action has reached its highest acceleration phase, and the powerful downbeat of the legs will combine with it to produce a greater velocity effect on the body. This propulsive factor in a forward direc tion also drives the hips up into a streamlined position. The total action therefore enhances streamlining and forward velocity.
- The streamlining factor is important, because the body must be parallel to the surface of the water for most of the propulsive phase to achieve the greatest speed.

In training, the undulating stroke would predominate with a major/minor kicking cycle. In competition, everything reverts to propulsion and streamlining with speed being the main consideration, and the leg action pattern will change to minor/major accordingly.

Another aspect of timing that must be considered is the relationship between the head and the hands. If the thumbs/hands enter the water before the head, then the undulation will be affected because the head movement plays a significant part in undulation: if the head does not enter the water first at this stage then a greater incline occurs, and profile resistance is also increased. This is a fault which is often detected among competitive swimmers as well as improvers; however, it is easily rectified by asking the swimmer which enters first, and then transposing the action accordingly – that is, with the head fractionally leading.

THE TEACHING AND EARLY COACHING OF BUTTERFLY STROKE

It is a mistake to try and coach the complete stroke in one short session; forward progression in the water will first be achieved by establishing an efficient leg action. It is important to demonstrate an emphatic hip movement – though a demonstration by the teacher on the pool side can be somewhat delicate. However, this can be overcome if both arms and hands are placed at the side of the hips and synchronized with the hip movement.

Once the leg action achieves undulation, both the kick-board and extended arms will counteract it to some extent. But if the arms are placed at the side and the leg action is attempted over short distances (5–10m), then an efficient level of undulation with progression forwards will be achieved. These practices over short distances (without the board) are enjoyable to the swimmer; there is no reactive effect, and he will find that he can soon produce a useful amount of forward-moving undulation.

Great difficulty is often experienced by young swimmers in the early stages as the arms go into the backward phase. However, it is quite possible to dispense with this stage until more important basics have been established. It is essential that they learn to use the body's levers efficiently. Young swimmers when bored tend to pike dive and touch the bottom of the pool; it is fun and easy, and in doing this they are unwittingly using the body as a series of levers in a most effective way. So why not make use of this and build it into a useful practice? All good 'flyers' speak of the 'flow' of the water over the body when they swim good 'fly' technique, and this has led to the 'flow fly' coaching and teaching principle, similar to the 'dive dolphin' techniques of old.

The 'flow fly' practice consists of a small dive into and under the water with the hands entering first, followed by the head (chin on chest) and body. Good depth is attained, then four dolphin movements take place with a sculling arm action and the head looking upwards; this brings the body back to the surface where the swimmer stops and stands up. It is important that the body's levers are used efficiently throughout. Thus the chin should go onto the chest so that the upper section of the head (above the hair line) enters the water first; if the flat portion of the face enters first, then there will be insufficient head movement. This practice should be repeated across the width, or the length of the pool, with the swimmer standing up or resting between each practice. Once undulation is established (with an efficient leg action), then the 'flow fly' practice can be alternated with, say, a throwing action from the standing position. It may be referred to as 'flow fly' and 'throw fly'.

The final step would be completion of the backward underwater phase and recovery of the arms over the water. Each step should be built up slowly, over days and even weeks, and the total level of skill will increase as the swimmer learns how each skill factor is obtained.

Whether the 'dive dolphin' or the 'flow fly' technique is used, swimmers should be made aware of how important the levers are, if they are to achieve depth and undulation.

Breath holding, too, is important, because when a swimmer progresses to full-stroke butterfly over short distances, it complements the body position and helps him concentrate on relating the recovery phase to the underwater sculling pattern.

The butterfly stroke is usually taught after the other three strokes have been mastered, but if undulation is taught earlier as a skill, then there is no reason why this stroke cannot be taught at an earlier stage.

Butterfly Drills

Drills	*Purpose*	*Teaching Points*
Butterfly Body Position		
1. Ascertained by position of hips (high)-push off from side, streamlined, then the leg action, arms at the side	Streamlining, then leg action for undulation	Stretch, then leg action; hips up, tummy down; feeling of flowing through the water
2. Breath holding	Streamlining	Breathe every 4/6 strokes
Butterfly Leg Action		
1. At the rail, leg action 4/6 only (very brief)	Comprehension of leg action	Hip movement: bottom up, tummy down
2. Arms at the side, leg action 1 width/10 metres on front	Arms at side gives greater undulation	Kick from hips *not* knees; point toes; keep feet together
3. Arms at side, leg action on the back	Progressive practice	Tummy up, bottom down
4. Leg action with body side-on, one arm extended, the other at the side	Progressive practice	Undulating arm movement assists body movement
5. Alternate extended arm	Progressive practice	
6. Leg action on the back arms locked and extended ahead	Progressive practice	
7. Leg action board/ outstretch arms/arms at side one deep, one shallow	Emphasis on one deep/one shallow	Be conscious of depth in the leg action
8. Use of flippers to enhance undulation	Forward progression and dolphin movement	
9. Flow fly practice, 4/6 legs only	Movement under the water	Drive into water; achieve depth, then 4/6 legs, stop and stand up

Drills	Purpose	Teaching Points
Butterfly Arm Action		
1. Flow fly practice	Teaches undulation and inward/outward sculling action	Thumbs enter; then head with chin to chest; get depth; 4 dolphin legs and sculling arm action to surface; stop
2. Use a throwing action with Flow fly	Progression only after achieving ability levels	As above
3. Press back now from brst arm action and throwing action into full stroke, 1 cycle only	Full stroke, 1 cycle only	Head down; hands close to water; brief practice only
4. Leg action; then brst arm action 2/4; then full stroke arm action 2/4; continue any sequence	Emphasis on the sculling radius; steady stroke build-up	Curb outward overscull, extend push phase; hand angles are constantly changing throughout
5. Leg action on the back with double arm backstroke action	Strengthening in recovery phase	
6. Legs with single arm 'catch-up', alternate arms	Concentration on sculling area	Sink to 'catch'; outward inward scull/backward push/recovery phases
7. Dolphin legs; no breathing for one third of pool with backs of hands touching, arms extended ahead	Closer entry position of the hands	Awareness of hand position at entry
8. As above, then full stroke	Awareness of hand entry	Entry concentration
Butterfly Breathing		
1. Dolphin legs with head hyper-extended	Awareness of head position	Inhalation concentration
2. Exhalation under the water/full stroke	Awareness of emptying lungs	
3. Breathing patterns 1 and 1; 2 and 1; 2 and 2; 3 and 2	Suitable cycle; race planning	Pattern to suit stroke cycle/cycles

Drills	*Purpose*	*Teaching Points*
Butterfly Timing For Head and Hands/Thumbs		
1. Full stroke over short distance	Timing for head and hands entry	Lower crown of head to enter before hands; chin to chest

4

The Back Crawl Stroke

Back crawl is ranked as the third fastest stroke after front crawl and butterfly and is similar to front crawl in that the alternating movement of the arms and the continual action of the legs create constant pressure on the water. However, the amount of power that can be exerted by the muscle groups used in this stroke is limited because of the swimmer being in a supine position (on his back). The backstroker must therefore have an exceptionally strong kick in order to enhance the propulsive factor of the arm action.

It is interesting to note that in the swimming laws there is no restriction concerning the arm and leg actions used, meaning that butterfly and/or breaststroke leg actions are both perfectly legal at any time throughout an event. Obviously those swimmers with a highly efficient dolphin kick will make full use of it during start and turn sequences, and it is excellent for those swimmers with superior timing and technique. The swimmer with an impeccable alternating leg action may, however, be better to employ this technique for any start and turn.

The law does state that a swimmer may not remain submerged for more than fifteen metres after a start and turn; by then his head must have broken the surface of the water.

THE BODY POSITION

An efficient body position may be summarized thus:

The general level of the water should be at or near the ear. The body is inclined, with the legs low enough in the water to give a good efficient kick. There are lateral movements due to the arm action in its outward scull; longitudinal movements also occur as the hand enters the water and goes for a deep 'catch'. The head is steady throughout, with the arm and leg action alternating and continuous.

There are no difficulties in this stroke concerning breathing and the immersion of the head in the water because except for the start and turn, the head is above the general water level throughout the distance that is swum. In the early stages the stroke can be taught with a float under each arm; the support these provide gives the beginner swimmer the confidence to progress to higher levels of proficiency.

As detailed above, lateral movements in this stroke result from the sideways 'fix' of the arms in the water. The arms cannot apply the pressure required to establish a 'fix' without support from the upper body; thus as they 'fix' on the water, the body reinforces this action by 'leaning' into the stroke. It is this

Fig 20a The body position of the improver swimmer leaves much to be desired; compare this with the streamlined position of the competitive swimmer in the next photograph.

Fig 20b Streamlined body position of the competitive swimmer in the back crawl stroke.

supportive action which is primarily responsible for any lateral movement, and it is controlled by an angular and efficient alternating leg action. Other factors which cause lateral movements in the stroke are:

1. A two- or four-beat leg kicking pattern.
2. An inefficient leg action, such as kicking from the knee.
3. 'Over-reaching' on entry.
4. 'Non-linear' recovery of the arm, as it traces an arc pattern from exit to entry.

5. A 'straight' arm action rather than a 'bent' arm action.

The six-beat leg action gives additional, continuous power to the stroke; combined with the arm action, it gives a propulsive thrust in a forward direction which helps to counteract lateral movement.

The movements around the longitudinal axis are created as the arms drop to a deep 'catch' and then press down in the conclusion of the 'push' phase. The head should remain steady and central throughout the stroke cycle; if it over-rolls it will contribute to both lateral and excessive longitudinal movements, neither of which is to be desired in the stroke. The head in a controlled position can help the swimmer concentrate on synchronizing the movement of the alternating levers.

THE LEG ACTION

An efficient leg action may be summarized thus:

The kick comes from the hip region, and acts down through the knee which bends in the movement upwards due to the pressure of the water and the timing of the levers for the propulsive phase. It finishes at the feet, which are pointed and whiplike with an angular movement. The maximum surface area of the foot is brought to bear on the water in both the up and down phases of the leg action. The kick is alternating and continuous, with the legs passing close to one another throughout.

Similar to the kicking action in front crawl, the leg action the in back crawl stroke achieves the following necessary functions:

1. It enhances the propulsive factor of the stroke (the arms being in a weaker position).

2. It is responsible for stabilizing the body position, because in the downward movement it achieves a 'bearing' area on the water which helps to maintain a streamlined body position. Moreover an efficient leg action helps to counteract the factors that create lateral movements: thus as the hand sinks to 'catch', the opposite leg kicks down, and this has a balancing effect on the related longitudinal movement, too. The degree of the latter is proportional to the amount of depth in the final 'push down', the entry of the opposite arm, and the efficiency of the leg action.

3. Describing the leg action as directly 'downwards' is not strictly accurate because the longitudinal roll of the body actually causes the path to be angular. Besides, if the leg action is inadequate some measure of body incline will occur, resulting in a proportional amount of profile resistance and therefore less forward progression.

4. Because the body is supine and therefore in a weaker position to exert power on the water, the leg action must work continuously with a six-beat pattern in order to assist propulsion. A swimmer with a lesser pattern or an inferior level of kicking efficiency will never achieve success in the higher competitive spheres of this stroke.

The Importance of the Foot

Some breaststrokers mix a dorsiflexed kicking action (backward) with the normal plantar-flexed position of the feet. However, if the feet are not efficiently plantar-flexed in back crawl then the propulsive factor is effectively reduced, even with a six-beat kicking pattern.

Plantar-flexion and flexibility of the feet at the ankle section are vitally important, not only for this stroke but for both front crawl and butterfly.

To test ankle flexibility, place a swimmer in a sitting position, plantar-flex the feet, and then measure from the toes to the floor level, taking the measurement from the point between the big toe and its neighbour. This test may not be clinically perfect, but it will indicate the improvement of flexibility levels over a period of time.

THE ARM ACTION

A good, efficient bent arm action may be summarized thus:

From the deep 'catch' position the hand flexes, then sculls outwards, backwards and upwards. When the arm is level with the head, the elbow starts to bend and continues to bend to an angle of 90 degrees. This brings the hand to within 15cm of the water surface; it continues to travel backwards, inwards and downwards and finishes well below the hip with the palm facing downward. It is then brought up to the water surface and exits from the water with the thumb or back of the hand leading. The arm is straight in the recovery phase, and re-enters the water with the little finger leading the hand ahead of the swimmer, in line with the shoulder. Assisted by the roll of the body, the hand drops to a deep 'catch'.

The 'Catch' Phase

A swimmer of high competitive calibre can reach 46cm in depth at the 'catch'. It is important to sustain depth at this stage because the body now starts to roll

Fig 21   Bent arm action in back crawl.

The Propulsive Phase

The hand should be angled at 30 or 40 degrees to ensure an effective 'fix' in the first stage of the propulsive phase. Except for hand flexion, the arm is virtually straight as it starts to travel upwards from 'catch'. When (outwardly) level with the head, the arm bends at the elbow (up to 90 degrees); we refer to this as the 'bent arm' action.

One good teaching point and practice is to instruct the younger 'age grouper' that, when the straight arm is level with the head, he should imagine that he is picking up a 'pie' and throwing it down to the bottom of the pool on every arm cycle; this achieves perfect bent arm technique. If the elbow starts to bend before it reaches the head then it will create a 'dropped elbow' problem: the result is

upwards; the elbow begins to bend at this point, the hand travelling upwards to the surface with the insweep of the arm action.

If the hand attains an efficient 'catch' at this initial stage, it will ensure a better 'fix' throughout the underwater phase of the arm action.

Fig 22a   The land-based drill showing the relative weakness inherent in the 'catch' position for the back crawl arm action.

Fig 22b   The elbows must not be higher than the hands midway through the arm action.

Fig 22c   The elbow is now positioned high behind the hand, where it should be in order to achieve maximum power for the final push down. The swimmer guiding the arms through the stroke pattern must provide reasonable support where the arm action is at its weakest, and adjust accordingly in the positions of strength.

loss of 'fix', and a detrimental effect on forward momentum.

A 'straight arm' action is when the arm is kept virtually straight throughout the underwater phase; however, this will lead to greater lateral movement in the stroke and the legs will have to work harder in order to regulate the situation. The 'straight arm' style still exerts a sculling path on the water because the rolling movement of the body optimizes the up-and-down movement of the arms in the underwater pattern.

The following exercise is one of the best land-based drills: one swimmer is seated whilst another stands behind him; the seated swimmer now moves through the bent arm propulsive phase with the standing swimmer guiding and providing reasonable support; he will manage some positions easily where the muscle groups are strong – for example in the final arm phase, that is, at 'push-down' – and will experience stress where they are weak, namely at 'catch' and the initial sculling pattern. This drill helps the swimmer to appreciate fully the value of finishing the arm action deep below the hip. It should also help to eradicate a 'dropped elbow' condition early in the propulsive phase of the stroke.

When demonstrating back crawl arm action, do not show the arm coming into the hip; even in the 'straight arm' action, the hand should finish well below the hip before recovery. A fully grown male international competitor may 'push through' to a depth of 60cm; this gives some idea of the depth necessary at 'catch' and in the final underwater phase of the arm action.

Some faults in technique that are seen in the entry and the propulsive phase of this stroke are:

1. Thumb entry and the arm bent at the elbow.

2. Back of the hand 'slapping' the water on entry.
3. A shallow 'catch'.
4. Little or no flexion after 'catch'.
5. Fingers open, giving little 'area of paddle'.
6. Shallow outsweep.
7. 'Dropped elbow' in the outward scull.
8. Weak or non-existent 'push-down'.

The Recovery Phase

Some world class swimmers can achieve propulsion during the downward and upsweep phase – just before the hand exits from the water – by adopting a wider-angled (wide of the hip) down-sweep. The blade of the hand is then brought around to face somewhat backwards (to the feet), and the final movement before exit is a sculling action that can contribute to the overall propulsive factor.

In the normal stroke cycle, the hand leaves the water with either the thumb leading, or the back of the hand (sometimes referred to as a 'broken hand' exit). If the final 'push down' is efficiently accomplished and the back of the hand exits, the hand has only to turn 90 degrees, so that the little finger can be presented on re-entry. If the thumb exits first, the 'blade' of the hand has to turn and achieve this position under the water.

The Entry Phase

If the entry of the arm isn't technically correct, it will create problems at 'catch' and lead to inefficiency in the early phase of the arm action. The variations of technique that can occur in the 'entry' phase are as follows:

1. The entry of the arm over the centre line.

2. The entry of the arm wide of the shoulder line.
3. Elbow bend at entry.
4. Entry by the back of the hand.
5. Little finger entry.

Back Crawl Sequence

The hand entering over the centre line leads to a lateral movement early in the arm action. If it enters wide of the shoulder line the area of the initial 'outsweep' will be reduced; and if it enters within the shoulder line and the

Fig 23a   As the little finger of the right hand enters the water, the left leg accelerates downwards, thereby controlling the longitudinal movement.

Fig 23d   Perfect harmony of movement between flexion of the hand, recovery of the left leg, and the right leg starting its drive downwards.

Fig 23b   Having achieved a 'fix' on the water, the arm now commences the outward sweep.

Fig 23e   The hand has come up to its highest point in the inward scull, the 'high elbow' position: it has come into line with the lower arm and away from the position of 'flexion'. The lower leg is at its lowest position in the drive down.

Fig 23c   As the outward sweep comes into line with the back of the head, there is increasing bend at the elbow. The flexion of the hand facing backwards (towards the feet) is in perfect balance with the continuing increase in the bend at the elbow.

Fig 23f   The arm now commences the downsweep with the hand 'leaning' into the movement.

Fig 23g   The arm continues in the downward sweep finishing well below the region of the hip. The final downsweep together with the entry of the left hand creates a longitudinal movement of the body.

Fig 23h   Completion of the longitudinal movement assists the right arm as it nears exit from the water. The hand 'rolls around' in this period of time in order to present the thumb or the back of the hand for exit.

Fig 23i   The recovery of the arm over the water is in a linear path. No bend should occur in the arm, and the entry should be within the width of the shoulder or in line with the ear.

elbow is bent, this can also create lateral movement. The greater consequence, however, is a 'dropped elbow' situation and reduced 'fix' early in the primary outsweep. If the back of the hand enters first, it fractionally reduces the amount of depth that is required for the 'catch' position; the hand then has to turn palm outwards, ready for the initial 'outsweep'. Any factor that minimizes these actions can reduce the efficiency of the 'catch' phase and early 'fix'.

In short, the hand entering the water with the little finger leading and in line with the shoulder will achieve the best results in the initial stages of the arm action.

BREATHING

Back crawl involves the easiest breathing sequence of any of the strokes, with inhalation on the recovery of one arm and exhalation as the opposite arm recovers. Some competitive swimmers will breathe every two arm cycles, and hypoxic breathing can take place every three, five or even seven cycles.

What should be remembered is that in all the competitive strokes, the breathing action assists the arm action with the muscles of respiration.

TIMING AND CO-ORDINATION

Good co-ordination in back crawl – as in the other strokes – relates to the number of kicking cycles there are to one complete arm cycle. A good efficient leg action is of paramount importance in back crawl since the body is supine and in a relatively weak position to exert the degree of power required from the arm action; the leg action must therefore add to the propulsive factor in every way possible. The most powerful leg-kicking pattern is the six-beat cycle (to one complete arm cycle) and all good back-strokers utilize it. Other types of kicking patterns are the two-beat and four-beat.

THE TEACHING AND EARLY COACHING OF BACK CRAWL STROKE

Back crawl is usually taught after the basics of front crawl have been established, although some teachers will introduce it as the third stroke after front crawl and breaststroke; this is to avoid the situation where plantar-flexion of the feet becomes so much ingrained in a swimmer's technique that he finds dorsi-flexion, which is necessary in breaststroke, difficult to achieve.

The main difficulty for the beginner in the early stages is achieving a streamlined supine body position; he is constantly nervous of 'over-rolling' which may result in his head going under the water. A confidence-giving remedy for this is to use two floats, one under each arm. Once he is a bit more competent, progressive leg action practices can continue, this time with two floats held closely to the chest; as ability and confidence grow, this can be reduced to one float.

The leg action practice where the body is supine and a float is held in extension above the head should be avoided for several reasons: it creates a certain degree of stress, and often leads to an unnatural, inclined body position. In many cases the head is also raised too high, causing the legs to sink and therefore creating profile resistance. Moreover the inefficiency of the leg action caused by this position is generally compounded by the swimmer adopting a type of cycling kicking action.

As the beginner becomes increasingly confident, his leg action technique will improve and this will lead to a more streamlined body position because the head will go back more; the optimum is when the water level reaches the ears. It is important to establish a decisive leg action in the early stages, and this is one occasion where a static land drill may be helpful before the arm action is introduced. There should be six kicks to one arm cycle, although many beginners find this difficult to accomplish at first. Nevertheless the basic target should be to achieve this level of efficiency, with a technique in which the legs are long and the feet plantar-flexed; the rest should then follow on.

The arm action should be taught as alternating and continuous, and it is important to use one-arm demonstrations for the arm action; a two-arm alternating demonstration can lead to 'duplication' difficulties and should only be attempted by the more proficient. Beginners find it hard to understand the 'bent arm' technique, and if it is badly taught it can lead to a 'dropped elbow' situation. A logical progressive step is to teach the 'straight arm' action first, and introduce the bent arm technique later on. Breathing will pose no problems.

When carrying out sectional work (arm action/leg action), it is essential that on completion of drill work the swimmer reverts to full stroke. And if paddles have been used during drill work, it is important to swim without them in order to get the 'feel' of the water back on the hands and arms.

There should always be a reason for a swimmer to use a particular drill. Drills are employed to improve technique, or to improve upon a certain fault in that technique. If this is not made clear to the swimmer, the drill becomes boring and does not achieve its purpose.

Back Crawl Drills

Drills	*Purpose*	*Teaching Points*
Back Crawl Body Position		
1. Ascertained by water to the ears and hip position (dish shape) with 2 floats, one in either hand, then kicking action	Gives balance and builds confidence with progression	Lean and hold on floats, water at ears; tummy pushed upward; look up to the ceiling
2. With float to chest push off then kicking	Streamlining and progression	Strong push off; keep head back and still
3. Float to chest; push, then 2 kicks	Progression to kicking action	Push, then kick slowly
4. Without float; arms sculling at side; push–glide–kick and scull (width)	Confidence drill without float	As above teaching points
5. 'Roll-over drill' arms extended and locked	Promotes rolling	Head steady in rolling movement; 10 kicks one side and 10 on the other
6. Full stroke and think about long body	Promotes better body position	Squeeze the bottom together
Back Crawl Leg Action		
1. Float to chest; push, then kick across width/s	Building leg action technique	Kick from hips; straight legs; point toes; tips of toes to come out of the water; kick closely together
2. Kicking on pool side	Promotes kicking technique	Kick comes from hips, not the knees
3. Without float; leg action width/s hands sculling at sides	Progressive practice assists leg action	Leg action to be continuous
4. Leg action arms at side	More purposeful kick	
5. 1/2 raised arms	Promotes stronger kick	

	Drills	*Purpose*	*Teaching Points*
6.	Extended and locked arms	Kick emphasis and promotes shoulder flexibility (advanced drill)	Keep arms straight; palm against palm; fingers inter-locked
7.	Elbows bent with hands on head	Arms create resistance to leg action	
8.	Kicking drill, hands on buttocks	Promotes better leg action	Deep leg kick
9.	Full stroke chin near chest	As above	Look at feet making a small splash

Back Crawl Arm Action

1.	Push/kick then build on arm cycles	Comprehension of arm action	Little finger entry; 'bury' hand in water; wrist flexion; sideways scull; push down below hips; thumb exit
2.	Leg action: 1 arm only, then other arm every 4/6/8 cycles (alter)	Reinforces arm comprehension	Little finger enters and thumb exits; fingers closed; arm straight in recovery by cutting a straight line in the ceiling
3.	Build on the arm cycles		
4.	Arms only, legs supported	Reinforces arm comprehension	
5.	Arms only, feet crossed or in inner tube	Resistance drill (advanced drill)	
6.	Single/double arm drills	Develops 'S' sculling	Scull to side, then in, and finish below hips
7.	'Throwing a pie'	Develops 'bent arm' technique	Arm straight until in line with head; pick up 'pie' and throw it down below the hips
8.	One arm extended ahead, other arm sculls/recovers and entry drill	Promotes arm entry	Enter in line with the shoulder

	Drills	Purpose	Teaching Points
9.	One arm at side, other in raised position then lowered to entry; repeated drill	Promotes straight recovery and in-line entry	Keep arm straight
10.	Alternating 'catch-up' drill; extended arm and alternate the arms	Promotes straight arm recovery and in-line entry	
11.	Paddle drill work	Develops the stroke muscle groups	

Back Crawl Breathing/Timing

1.	Breathing practices to one-arm cycle	Comprehension of breathing cycle	Teaching demonstration; breathe in on one arm and out the other
2.	As one arm enters count number of leg kicks before re-entry	Creates efficient timing	6 leg kicks to one complete arm cycle

Breaststroke

Breaststroke is certainly the oldest of the four competitive strokes, and it is the most popular stroke amongst social swimmers, probably because the head can be above the surface of the water all the time, with constant visual contact in the immediate area. The main problem is that the badly taught social swimmer will 'screw kick' to some degree; this reduces the propulsive effect of the kicking action and if it is not corrected the problem will become established to the detriment of both the stroke and the swimmer.

GENERAL TECHNIQUE

The stroke has had many modifications. Regarding the leg action, the width between the knees in the recovery phase varies between individual swimmers. If the recovery to the hips is very wide, then the drive backwards will be with the wedge-like sole of the foot, and because of this it is called a 'wedge kick'. Whereas if the knees are closer together, a greater part of the lower leg will contribute in the action backward; this is known as a 'whip kick', and is referred to as either a narrow or a wide whip kick depending on how close together the knees are in the recovery phase. The total action in the whip kick is quicker than in the wedge sequence, as recovery and the propulsive phase is faster. The action of the feet also contributes to the overall effect in speed, as the feet 'spin' outwards (dorsiflex) with a fast whip-like movement.

In the sixties Chet Jastremski lowered world records by using a more streamlined stroke. In his personal technique his leg action was less efficient than his arm action, so he developed a low angular body profile with an arm-dominated stroke; a higher body position would have created more outline resistance, a factor he could ill afford. The lower angular position ensured a streamlined body position, so speed and propulsion were proportionately maximized to the level of efficiency in his leg action. As a result of his success at world level, many copied the Jastremski style and argued in its defence, but without realizing the reasoning behind it. In Europe, however, breaststroke swimmers adopted a higher body position, and as a consequence of the difference in styles, breaststroke became known for a time as the 'American'-type breaststroke or the 'European'. At the present time, all international breaststroke is swum with a high body position, for reasons that are explained below.

THE BODY POSITION ————————

An efficient body position may be summarized thus:

When the arms and legs are fully extended the body is horizontal with the head pillowed between the arms. The body undulates throughout the whole phase of the stroke cycle. Unless there is a glide component within the stroke cycle, the head and arm actions are continuous, with the arms and legs co-ordinating in their movements throughout.

The streamlined position should be horizontal to the general surface of the water, and a breaststroker with good technique will pillow the head between the arms as he recovers forwards. The recreational or social swimmer keeps the chin on, or clear of the water throughout the recovery of the arms forwards; this creates an inclined body position and therefore additionally increases profile resistance.

After the arm recovery the feet are plantar-flexed, and some of the higher calibre swimmers will tuck the sole of one foot into the instep of the other (similar to the front crawl two-beat crossover position) at extension to improve streamlining. Like this, the position of the head and feet achieves perfect streamlining of the body. Other swimmers are content to conclude the kicking action just by bringing both feet together as closely as possible.

Speed is the major consideration to the competitive swimmer, and in this respect there have been many arguments as to the optimum angle the upper body should assume during the insweep stage of the arm cycle: it was found that the flatter body position created less resistance, but in a higher position the power that could be created by the muscle groups of the upper body was relatively greater – the arms could be brought closer into the body so the power of the pectorals, lats and other muscle groups could be concentrated more effectively on the insweep of the arms. Some swimmers misunderstand the reasoning behind the higher body position and adopt it without making the vigorous effort required in the arm action. Consequently their input of power to the insweep of the arms is minimal, yet they continue to bob up and down relatively upright, creating a situation of needless resistance for themselves.

There are two types of upper body action which swimmers may adopt as they sink once more to the streamlined position. The first is an undulating action created by ducking the chin into the chest, synchronized with the movement of the hands as they extend forwards; the head is pillowed between the upper arms and altogether this head movement creates a dolphin-like undulating movement of the upper body. In the other type of action, the head remains in line with the upper body throughout. The undulating movement is a two-lever movement involving the head and upper body; the in-line position is a one-lever movement. The two-lever action will create a greater degree of undulation, which does more to help progression through water.

Knowing the value of undulation, some coaches tried to integrate this into the stroke with dolphin-like movements in the leg action. Thus leg action drills used to combine both the normal simultaneous leg action with that of the dolphin leg action; as a result, certain swimmers finished the latter phase of the leg action with a pronounced dolphin-like movement. This led to many confrontations with officialdom and subsequent disqualifications. If the very necessary undulation is to be brought into the training and competitive environment, it should be cultivated from the forward extremity and not the rear, and achieved by synchronizing the head action with the movement of the hands after completion of the insweep (see section The Arm Action).

As the body comes to a 'gradual' height in the water, there is also a proportional 'gradual' recovery of the legs. This recovery process of the legs only reaches completion as the arms are in the extension phase forwards and the body is again dropping downwards. Many assume that when the body is in this high position, the upper leg is also at full recovery. However, if this were so, it would indeed create a high factor of resistance. It must be remembered that with the competitive swimmer the body and leg angles are constantly changing and that each progressive stage is so well coordinated that as one angle is at maximum, the other is rapidly diminishing.

In the case of the untutored or social swimmer, there is always some degree of body incline throughout the breaststroke cycle. The recovery of the upper leg to the navel is almost, and at times in excess of, 180 degrees, and under these circumstances both profile resistance and to a certain extent eddy current resistance would be created by the angle of the upper leg. The talented competitive swimmer, on the other hand, will adopt both streamlined and angular body positions, with the upper legs recovering to an angle of efficiency of approximately 140 degrees; as a result the water flows under the contours of the body and down the constant sloping changes of the upper leg. The propulsive phase of the leg action starts as the arms are two-thirds of the way through to full extension, and so the body is almost streamlined during the major part of the leg drive backwards.

In the position of ultimate streamlining, the water flows over the arms, over the head which is tucked in between the upper arms, over the lower body and finally away from the feet which are plantar-flexed and in a position of accord.

THE LEG ACTION

An efficient leg action may be summarized thus:

From an extended position, the knees progressively bend until the upper leg recovers (within hip width) approximately 140 degrees to the main trunk. The feet now dorsiflex and drive outwards, backwards, downwards and then inwards until they come together in a plantar-flexed position.

The leg action in breaststroke is mainly propulsive although the downward phase will also contribute – albeit nominally – to the streamlining of the body position; this contribution occurs in the latter phase, in the dolphin-like movement after the backward drive. During the main propulsive phase of the leg action, the upper body is in a position of streamlining with the arms moving to extension ahead. Due to this streamlined body position, the power in the backward leg action creates greater forward progression than that generated by the arm action. During the arm cycle, the increasingly rising upper body creates a progressive resistance factor, and the power developed by the arm action must be sufficient to overcome this angular drag effect and still create adequate forward progression.

In both the whip and the wedge kick, the legs are recovered to the lower trunk where the feet then dorsiflex. The action of dorsiflexion (when performed by a reasonably able swimmer) is the fastest single limb movement in any of the four competitive strokes; a proficient breaststroker has extremely flexible ankles and exceptionally 'fast feet'. However, dorsiflexion of the feet creates most of the problems in this stroke. In the early beginner stages it must be emphasized to all swimmers that they must turn the feet out in the kick-back; many swimmers will even plantar-flex with one foot and dorsiflex with the other.

The leg action traces out a circular pattern before the feet finally come together and make contact. The beginner may first attempt dorsiflexion with the toes curled downwards during the semi-circular, 180-degree kicking action; but if the circular leg action were to continue in ever-increasing circles, the foot would spiral downwards like the thread of a screw – hence the expression 'screw kick'. This condition may also be caused by one hip being lower than the other. The 'screw kick' is not easy to eradicate, for true

dorsiflexion can only be achieved with the toes 'curled' upwards towards the shin. This is a great teaching point, and one that has clarified the action of dorsiflexion for many swimmers.

Learning how to turn the feet outwards is a major problem in this stroke. Static land drills serve no useful purpose unless it is to waste time in the lesson. One method that has been successful, however, is accomplished using two rubber bands ('band-Joes'), one fitted round the lower leg, and the other round the big toe (See Figs 24a, 24b and 24c).

Many an untutored swimmer manages breaststroke with the feet pointed. However, this does nothing for the propulsive phase of the stroke, except by minimally helping to keep the hips up.

The two types of leg action associated with this stroke are the whip kick and the wedge kick.

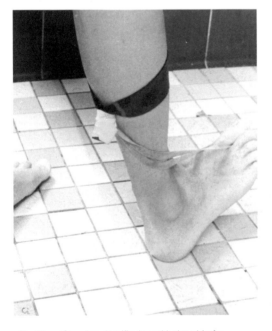

Fig 24a   Showing dorsiflexion with the aid of a 'band-Joe'.

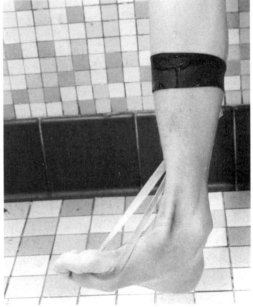

Fig 24b   Dorsiflexion with the band under the big toe.

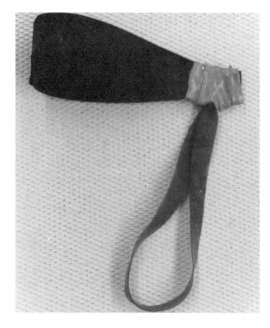

Fig 24c   The two bands connected together. Simple to construct, yet achieving a high rate of success.

The Whip Kick

All proficient life savers use the whip-kick technique, although in life saving it is referred to as the 'inverted breaststroke kick'. The action is exactly the same as that used in whip-kick technique and in fact the inverted kicking technique is excellent for competitive whip-kick sectional practices. A further progressive kicking practice is for one breaststroker to tow another on his back with his knees bent; this creates an excellent overload drill. The swimmers change over every 50m.

It is easier for the teacher and coach to identify whether the swimmer is using whip or wedge technique if he is viewed from behind. The important thing to look for is the width between the knees; if the knees are exceptionally wide apart, and if the soles of the feet are facing backwards, the position indicates a wedge kick. The width between the knees is the identifying factor, whether the kick is whip or wedge. With whip kicks there are wide whip kicks and narrow ones: in a narrow whip kick the knees are close together and in a vertical line under the hips. The feet are dorsiflexed, and initially both the lower limb and the inside of the foot unite to form a compounding area of lever in the drive backwards.

In the kicking action the feet are working constantly as they scull backwards, outwards, downwards then inwards. A

Fig 25
Breaststroke leg action 'drag drill'.

Fig 26   Breaststroke leg actions: Fig 26a (top) shows a wide whip kick; Fig 26b (bottom) shows a narrow whip kick.

proficient kicker has the co-ordination and ability to finish the inward circular scull with the feet nestling into each other; less efficient kickers will trace out the shape of a parabola with a straight-lined base. The first part of the leg action is circular, with the legs then squeezing together on the inward phase; and some degree of knee angle must be maintained for the inward scull. Failing this, the legs will come together too soon, achieving little in propulsion.

The leg action accelerates throughout, with the feet constantly fixing and moving in every range of angular movement. The kick must be circular, even though the knee is a hinged joint incapable of any outward movement. After flexion and recovery to the hips, this circular movement is accomplished by the following synchronized actions:

1.   The femur (upper leg) is drawn (minimally) outwards by the hip abductors.
2.   Dictated by this action of the femur, the knees also travel (minimally) outwards with the feet moving inwards.
3.   The femur next starts to be drawn inwards by the hip adductors, and in the same action the feet now dorsiflex and so 'catch' and gain a 'fix' on the water throughout the rest of the cycle.
4.   The knee now starts to extend (in unison with the adduction of the femur and lower leg) with the extending leg progressively being drawn inwards.
5.   Automatic rotation complements the final phase of the circular movement, with the femur rotating inwards and bringing the feet together on plantar-flexed extension.

The hip abductors and adductors are together responsible for the extension of the knee and hip to achieve the necessary semi-circular action. If a swimmer places sideways pressure on the knee joint to achieve this action, then damage will result to the knee joint and ligaments. A coach must be aware of this complex sequence of movement because this knowledge can forestall many of the knee problems we sometimes come to accept as the norm in breaststroke.

The Wedge Kick

So called because the 'wedge-like' sole of the foot presses backwards on its own, with minimal supportive 'bearing area' (on the water) from the lower leg. The knees are recovered wide of the hips, then driven outwards, backwards, downwards and inwards. The range of sculling movement is wider but with a slower tempo than that of the whip kick. Because the knees are placed outwards (they are wide of the hips) and in the direction of movement, the likelihood of damage to the knee joint is diminished.

If the leg action is to be efficient, the semi-circular sculling path must always take place. Once the whip-kick technique is explained and demonstrated, a swimmer should have little difficulty in adapting from the wedge to the whip kick.

Fig 27   The wedge kick.

ARM ACTION

An efficient bent elbow arm action may be summarized thus:

From the extended forward position, the hands flex to an angle of 30 degrees. The arms then sweep outwards, backwards and downwards, assuming a 'high elbow' position at the completion of the outward scull. They now scull inwards with the hand angles constantly changing in order to maintain a 'fix' on the water throughout the cycle. Near completion of the inward scull, the fingertips almost meet with the hands facing slightly upwards. On extension forwards, they spiral around and face palm downwards, then outwards as they reach full extension and 'catch'. The arms accelerate in

their action throughout the complete movement.

There are two types of arm action associated with this stroke: the bent arm action and the straight arm action. The **bent arm action** is associated with the competitive swimmer and is synonymous with that of the whip-kick leg action. It is usual to see the straight arm action adopted by the social type of swimmer. Obviously the turn-over rate of the straight arm technique is less than that of the bent arm action and would complement the slower wedge-kick leg action.

The Catch Phase

The 'catch' in breaststroke is minimal in depth (approximately 15cm). If, however, the arm action is co-ordinated with an undulating pattern in the extension, then the 'catch' will be deeper. The hands then flex and 'fix' onto the water.

The Propulsive Phase

The hands move outwards, downwards and backwards with the elbows gradually bending until they assume an angle of 90 degrees (high elbow). As the hands complete the outward scull, the fingers at this stage are pointing downwards to the bottom of the pool. The hands must now turn for the inward sweep, their position changing from palm out to palm in (approximately 130–140 degrees); it is an action best described as being like the circling of the hand inside a large jam jar. This is where the 'fix' on the water can be interrupted or even lost.

An efficient inward sweep accounts for the highest amount of forward propulsion. Many swimmers have difficulty in establishing the correct hand angles for the important inward phase, and as a consequence the hands are turned a mere 90 degrees, then 'slice' together with loss of both 'fix' and propulsion. The 'turning of the corner' from the outward to inward sweep should be continually scrutinized by the coach. The angular pattern now continues inwards, from the fingers pointing down at the high elbow position until they come together on completion of the insweep. At this point the hands are held palms upward. The sweep continues as the hands enter extension and rotate as they proceed to full extension, by which time the palms will be facing outwards. A successful teaching point is to instruct the student to 'open the book, then close the book' because it achieves the correct hand angles at completion of the insweep and commencement of the extension.

The straight arm action consists of a long, sculling action outwards. The main problem is that the swimmer will either lose, or reduce, the proportion of 'fix' on the water as the hands rotate inwardly at the commencement of the insweep. At this moment the elbows must bend in order to bring the hands inwards. If a level of efficiency is to be maintained, the hand angles should relate to the inward sweep technique in the bent arm action.

There are common faults in both actions, but the two that give rise to concern on the part of the competitive swimmer are:

1. The loss of 'fix' when 'turning the corner'.
2. The dropping of the elbows in the inward sweep.

'Dropping the elbows' compromises the ability to use the powerful upper body muscle groups, so the level of forceful acceleration is curtailed. Many social swimmers continue the outward movement past the shoulders, finishing in the region of the hips. When this occurs there can be no inward phase, and a period of resistance with zero propulsion is created in the time that the hands are brought forwards to extension.

Breaststroke Sequence

Fig 28a   As the feet come together the arms are fully extended, with the hands in the 'catch' position.

Fig 28b   Both hands now start to flex, so achieving an early 'fix' on the water.

Fig 28c   The outward sweep continues until wide of the shoulders.

Fig 28d   After circling in, the hands commence the insweep phase. The body starts to rise for the breathing cycle to take place, and also to allow the powerful muscles of the upper body to assist the arm action.

Fig 28g   The position of the legs indicates an efficient whip kick. The feet now dorsiflex, the knees move outwards (the influence of the abductor muscles), and the body is propelled forwards with the feet and lower legs 'fixing' and driving backwards through the water.

Fig 28e   As the fingers almost touch, the feet are recovered to the hips.

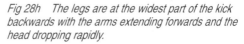

Fig 28h   The legs are at the widest part of the kick backwards with the arms extending forwards and the head dropping rapidly.

Fig 28f   At this moment in the arm action, explosive inhalation takes place.

Fig 28i   The hands/arms and head synchronize in movement to trace a spiralling path, downwards then upwards to extension, creating the necessary undulation of the body in this phase of the stroke.

Fig 28j The feet are driven backwards and downwards, a 'fix' on the water still being achieved by the lower legs and feet.

Fig 28k The feet plantar-flexed and close together, 'moulding' one into the other.

Fig 28l The arms at full extension with the hands turned ready to flex into the next outsweep. The head is tucked between the biceps and the body is perfectly streamlined, in the optimum position to achieve velocity and progression from the leg action.

BREATHING

There are no problems associated with this action, except if the head is in a raised position during the propulsive phase of the leg action. Exhalation takes place throughout the underwater phase of the stroke, with the major function occurring immediately before the head sinks down beneath the water. Inhalation occurs as the head is rising to the high body position (competitive stroke).

When a positive movement takes place in weight training, vigorous inhalation is an important contributory function because it oxygenates the respiratory muscles – the intercostals and the diaphragm – and controls the flow of blood in an upward path, and so on. This normal function can also be exploited in breaststroke to assist the powerful upper body muscles in controlling the arms which create forward propulsion. If the head moves from a position of low profile resistance, then it must be returned to that same position. The more proficient competitive breaststroker not only 'pillows' the head down between the arms, he also 'hunches' the shoulders inwardly (almost touching the ears); this is the position of minimum profile body resistance.

TIMING AND CO-ORDINATION

Every action takes its place in logistical order: thus, pull – breathe – kick for the competitive swimmer, and pull – breathe – kick and glide for the social type of swimmer. Nothing could be simpler you may say; however, despite its apparent simplicity, co-ordinating the stroke has troubled more than a few teachers and coaches, and has affected even the best of swimmers. Speed and efficiency in this stroke relate to the timing of the arm and leg actions: one action should be completed before the other 'takes effect', and the line of demarcation is wafer thin. If one action overrides the other, it will result in a degree of propulsive inactivity, and forward progression will be affected. If co-ordination is very bad – a swimmer who pulls and kicks at the same time – the lack of forward momentum will result in a certain degree of depth; in short he will sink!

The fastest that man can travel in water (front crawl) is approximately five miles an hour (8kph); in breaststroke the speed is proportionally slower, so it is imperative for the timing to be exact; any hiccup in its efficiency will result in a corresponding loss of forward progression. The extensive use of over-distance, full-stroke training routines (400s, 600s and even 800s) is sometimes included in schedules for the competitive breast-stroker. However, in order to complete the distance or set, the swimmer must adopt a more streamlined body position, and this lower body position can have detrimental results in the co-ordination of the stroke when the swimmer reverts to the higher body position. For this reason, over-distance full-stroke training routines should be carefully considered and monitored.

The timing in breaststroke concerns the completion of the leg action (plantar-flexion, or the feet meeting together) and the position of the arms in their action. As the feet come together, the hands should be moving from 'catch' and flexion. If the efficiency in the timing is affected, then separate the leg action and arm action with a 'glide' movement. When better co-ordination has been established, use 'building' sets in the schedule, gradually increasing the distance, pace and the stroke rate with 'target times' on the swim sets.

THE TEACHING AND EARLY COACHING OF BREASTSTROKE ——

The foremost objective is to achieve a reasonable leg action, and any difficulties encountered in this region can only be overcome by patience and good progressive teaching practices. Static land drills, where the feet are pulled and moved into positions of dorsiflexion, achieve little that is helpful. Coaches must also beware that initial practices do not place too much emphasis on the arm action, otherwise the beginner will adopt a plantar-flexed (pointing the toes) position of the feet in the early stages of learning, and difficulties will be met later on in leg practices which require the feet to turn out.

As when teaching butterfly, be careful when using the expression 'kicking' or 'kick back'. If a footballer plantar-flexes his foot when he kicks a ball, he ends up by 'toe-punting' it. If he wishes to place the ball, he hits it with his intep and this ensures a good degree of dorsiflexion. Teachers and coaches must therefore be aware of the significance of the expression, particularly while teaching leg action in breaststroke. In butterfly the main object is to attain a movement from the hips; in breaststroke the object is to 'push back' with the feet turned out; the expression 'kick back' could lead to an undesirable degree of plantar-flexion.

Some success has been achieved with beginners sitting on the side of the pool with the feet in the water; the teaching points were 'to bend the knees, turn the feet out and push backwards in a round circle'. Initial water practices include the 'inverted' breaststroke position with a float under each arm and teaching points when required; it is important that the knees do not come above the surface of the water because if they do they will recover beyond 180 degrees in the actual stroke in the 'on-breast' position.

Another exercise is to hold the rail and attempt leg action in the 'on breast' body position; then practise the leg action holding a float with the arms, but only over short distances. It should be remembered that 'on breast' leg action practices are difficult while holding a float because there is a low level of efficiency in the leg action at this early stage and the inclined body position on the float creates resistance. So it is essential only to practise over short distances in the early stages until dorsiflexion of the feet is instinctively automatic.

The arm action is easier to instil with the teaching point of 'pull in small circles', and there are many others that may suit the requirements of the teacher. However, note that arm-only practices with a float held between the legs achieve little in the way of progression because the beginner tends to relax the adductor muscles and so loses the float; therefore the practice is constantly interrupted. Using full stroke over short distances, then increasing the distance, would appear to be the best progressive arm practice. The breathing cycle is often ignored, but it is very important in that it helps the swimmer to achieve full extension of the arms and a more streamlined body position. An inclined body position is always a problem in the early stages; if the swimmer can learn to lower the head behind the hands as he exhales – 'blow away the hands' – he will immediately achieve greater streamlining with less profile resistance. Also, after forceful exhalation the swimmer must vigorously inhale, which takes place during the arm cycle. This complements a higher body position, with the respiratory muscles assisting the muscles of the upper body in the arm movements. This teaching point can also be used to good effect in the coaching aspects of the stroke.

It is important to emphasize the advantages of the glide in the early stages; the glide ensures an adequate range of movement in the leg and arm action, and it also slows down the swimmer and establishes correct co-ordination in the stroke.

Drills	*Purpose*	*Teaching Points*
Breaststroke Body Position		
1. Holding float, push off; glide; hold breath then chin on water	Streamlining	Stretch out, look along the float
Breaststroke Leg Action		
1. Sitting on pool side with feet in water	Partial comprehension of the leg action	Make anti-clockwise circles; turn toes up, feet outwards; bend at knee; feet to come together
2. In the water, one hand on rail, the other on wall with fingers pointing	Comprehension of the leg action	Kick back with the heel
3. Two floats, one under each arm, supine with inverted leg action		Make circles with the heels
4. On breast, hand-held float, push and glide 2/3 leg cycles and *build*		
5. Hands at hips, recovery kick to touch hands	Greater range of movement	
6. Introduce a long glide after extension	Creates more powerful leg and arm action; also restores timing	Pull, breathe, kick and count three in the glide
7. Hands clasped behind the back	Advanced technique	
8. On the back with arms held vertically upward	Advanced technique	Arms straight up, upper leg parallel to water surface
9. Supine with arms extended ahead and hands interlocked	Shoulder flexibility	Arms straight with hands locked together
10. One normal leg action, 1 dolphin leg action; vary sequence	Promotes undulation	Extend undulating rhythm

Drills	*Purpose*	*Teaching Points*
11. One width/length lung burster; mini arm cycle extension ahead and leg action	Promotes greater range of movement	Greater range of dorsiflexion and feet to crossover at full extension
12. Towing partner drills with bent knees	Advanced technique	Straight arms; grip hands

Breaststroke Arm Action

1. Standing practice in shallow water	Comprehension of the arm action	Make small circles scull outwards, backwards, downwards, inwards; keep hands within view; smooth extension ahead
2. Push and glide, then 2/3 arm cycles, *build* after progression	Concentration on arm action	Full stroke, short distances only
3. Walking into 'collapse' onto breast; *build* full stroke cycles		Two paces, then full stroke; concentration on arm action
4. Arms only, legs in pull buoy	Advanced technique	Keep the scull in front of the shoulders
5. Two arm cycles, one leg cycle		
6. Single alternate arm cycle, legs in pull buoy		Continuous circular arm action
7. Right hand sculling, other holds right ankle; alternate each length	Develops efficient sculling pattern	Keep continuous sculling action
8. Full stroke arm action, legs in pull buoy	Concentration on arm action	Think continuous hand sculling patterns
9. Undulating recovery with dolphin leg action	Promotes undulation	Waveform recovery with head following arm pattern
10 Weighted hand paddles	Overloads the arm muscle groups	

Drills	Purpose	Teaching Points
11. Towing partner drill; one swimmer arms only, the other is towed	Advanced technique	One partner grips ankles of the swimmer, then bends knees to 180 degrees

Breaststroke Breathing

Drills	Purpose	Teaching Points
1. 'Blow the hands away' drill	Ensures lower head and good exhalation	Dip the head behind the thumbs
2. Breathing cyclical drill	Ensures timing in breathing	Inhale as hands come together and exhale as the arms extend ahead

Timing In Breaststroke

Drills	Purpose	Teaching Points
1. Glide after extension	Ensures timing	Hold the glide position
2. Glide counting drill		Count 3 in the glide position
3. Full stroke drill		After the feet touch look for the hands just moving apart

6

Competitive Starts

It appears there is a diversity of opinion as to how much time and in-depth instruction should be devoted to starting procedures. In many cases only cursory attention is paid to the techniques involved, mainly because the time taken to accomplish any start is relatively short compared to that taken by the race itself. There are, however, two considerations that must be uppermost: one is that the vast majority of coaches are dealing with an age group programme; and secondly, an efficient start creates rapid momentum into the stroke.

An effective start should create a velocity through the air of three times the swimming speed. If, however, the swimmer's trajectory is too vertical, but still with a streamlined entry, then the start will be much too deep. Conversely if his trajectory is too horizontal, he will flatten out on the water and this will create resistance to forward momentum. A good starting technique depends on the velocity of upward movement, the correct movement of the levers in flight (which transfers momentum to the axis of the body) and a streamlined entry. Moreover, if both the degree of power and the direction are correct, then the resultant velocity on entry will have a considerable effect on the first 10 or 15m of a race.

The early part of an age group swim-

ming education is first and foremost a 'learning' programme. Good techniques learned at this stage become ingrained in later stages, and it is during this period that techniques in strokes, starts and turns must be a major part of the itinerary. A swimmer should be introduced to the varying methods, he should be able to identify and practise the different techniques, and he can then capitalize on this acquired expertise in competition. The various starts we see in competition are as follows:

- The grab start
- The pike start
- The hitch-kick start
- The track start
- The relay take-over start
- The back crawl start

SOME RELATIVE MECHANICAL PRINCIPLES

In order to capitalize on the flight phase of a competitive start, some basic mechanical principles should be understood. First, the centre of gravity is the body's weight centre, and this is roughly in the pit of the stomach, 3cm in front of the spine. When a person stands upright, if an imaginary line is drawn from the weight centre to between the feet, that person is in a position of balance and will not fall over.

During starting procedures, when the chin is raised, the body inclines forwards and the weight is transferred from the flat of the foot to the ball of the foot. The centre of gravity will now move outwards, away from the perpendicular line, the body falls forwards and the leg drive takes place. Once the body is in flight a certain degree of rotation takes place around the centre of gravity; this is due to the Earth's gravitational pull, and it is a force which acts on the body at all times.

The body must now follow a parabolic path (see Fig 29) which takes the swimmer into the water. If the head and arms observe the correct angular movements, the body follows the line of the parabola and enters the water cleanly. If, however, a swimmer throws the arms too high above the head when in flight, his back will arch when he is still in the air and he will 'belly flop' onto the water. The legs are responsible for propelling the body into flight, and the head and arms assist its trajectory by transferring movements of momentum to it. More important still, if the movements of the head and arms

are directional, the flight path will be directional; for example, when the head and arms move downwards in flight, the hips can 'pike' more easily and the body will follow the line of flight downwards.

Kinetic energy is the energy of motion of a body or system; its proper definition is that it is 'equal to the product of half its mass and the square of its velocity'. In practical terms it is useful in any start technique. For example, during an arm swing in a forward direction there is a build-up of energy; if the arm swing is stopped suddenly, a transfer of momentum occurs in the same direction as the swing before it was stopped. This theory can be applied successfully to any circular arm movement, as in the 'wind-up start' when momentum is transferred to the body as it moves forwards.

Similarly, the way in which the body's mass (the size of it) is distributed is known as a 'moment of inertia'. Thus when a swimmer extends in flight, the moment of inertia is large about the transverse axis (see Fig 30); but when he tucks into a ball, the moment of inertia is small in the region of the transverse axis, as in the hitch-kick start, and this creates faster rotation around the body's radius.

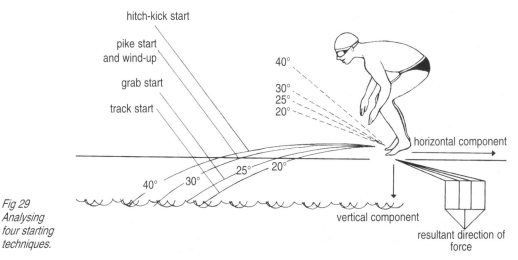

Fig 29
Analysing
four starting
techniques.

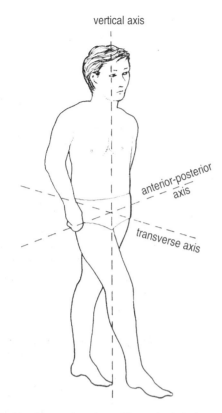

vertical axis

anterior-posterior axis

transverse axis

Fig 30   Centre of gravity and lines of axis in the body.

No matter which start a swimmer may decide upon or how difficult the technique associated with the start, the over-riding consideration will always be the speed of the individual's reflexes. Thus the swimmer must react instantly to the initial component of the signal which her-alds the start. Young age-groupers should be told that there are three components to the bang of the starter's pistol, as thus: b – a – ng. A swimmer with instantaneous reactions goes on the 'b'.

THE READY POSITION

In any competitive start, the referee will give a warning blast on the whistle with a

signal to get up on the blocks or enter the water. For any start that entails mounting a starting block, many swimmers adopt a 'bent over' position before the instruction to 'take your marks'; like this they claim they can see the content of the starting block and the height from the water at the same time and can gauge how much effort is required for the starting sequence.

When analysing a start, the major points for clarification are the stance; the take-off; the flight; and finally the entry and transition into the stroke.

THE GRAB START

The grab start is so called because the swimmer crouches over the front edge of the starting block and takes a firm grip on it. The thumbs should 'support' the other fingers of each hand by gripping and not pressing down on the block; should the thumbs press down on the block they will act to balance the body. Assuming that the angle of the legs is correct between the upper and lower limb (approximately 140 degrees), this balancing action is unnecessary. Furthermore if the thumbs press down on the block they will also compromise the initial upward action of the arms in the 'take-off' stage.

During the 'take-off' phase in the grab start, the swimmer should theoretically pull on the block in an upward direction until the body is pulled forwards to a point of no return. However, swimmers now prefer to move the arms rapidly for-wards and then stop them suddenly because the transfer of momentum assists the forward motion of the body so ensur-ing a fractionally faster start.

An efficient grab start will give an inclined velocity which is ample for the normal club swimmer. Once the tech-niques have been mastered and applied

Fig 31a   The toes are over the edge of the block with the feet hip-width apart. The hands grip the block inside/outside the feet. The upper leg is at an angle of 140 degrees to the lower leg.

over a period of time, then the swimmer should progress to the pike start.

Stance

The swimmer comes forwards from the 'ready' position and the toes grip the front edge of the block, hip-width apart. The hands grip the block either between or to the side of the feet; the thumbs give support alongside the first finger – they should not be placed on the top edge of the block. The head is lowered so the eyes look backwards. The angle between the upper and lower leg should be approximately 140 degrees: if it is as much as 180 degrees there is a tendency to topple forwards because the weight of the body is forwards; if the knee bend is too much,

Fig 31b   The head now moves forwards, followed by the hands as they extend ahead. As the weight of the body is transferred to the balls of the feet, the body is moved forwards to a point of no return.

Fig 31d   Both head and arms move downwards to form the forward angular position, the head pillowed between the biceps for entry. This movement commits the body to the downward arc of the parabola.

Fig 31c   The body now launches into a semi-circular path with the head moving downwards from a forward-looking position. The body is stretched and streamlined.

Fig 31e   As the fingertips touch the surface of the water, the arms move forwards once more, thus creating a 'hole' through which the rest of the body follows.

the arms will be used to anchor the body in position to stop it toppling backwards. Some swimmers position themselves in an excessively forward angle on the blocks, but this places an intolerable strain on muscle groups which as a consequence use vital reserves of energy before they are even in flight.

Take-off

When the signal to start is given the head should almost immediately move forwards in a combined movement with the hands which release their hold on the block and also thrust forwards. The weight of the body transfers from the flat sole to the ball of the foot. These simultaneous actions move the body outwards to a point of no return; the knees then straighten and propel the body forwards and upwards.

Flight

The body is launched into a semi-circular path. The head moves rapidly downwards, the chin tucking into the chest, the eyes looking backwards. The arms are lowered from the forward angular position so the head is now pillowed between them for entry. Like this the body is now committed to the downward phase of the parabola.

Entry

As the fingertips touch the surface of the water the arms angle forwards once again; this has a reverse piking effect on the hips so that the trailing legs come into line with the upper body. The fingertips enter first, creating a 'hole' in the water through which the rest of the body may follow. As soon as the head has entered, it follows the path of the arm movement

forwards and upwards, thus assisting the body to straighten and come into line. Experience alone teaches co-ordination and speed in these movements which are calculated so the body achieves, as quickly as possible, a path which is parallel to the surface of the water.

Transition into the Stroke

After a brief period of glide, the arms, head, body and legs are perfectly streamlined. The glide is held until the momentum of the entry diminishes to swimming speed. In front crawl the relative number of leg cycles to one arm stroke and the raising of the head takes the swimmer to the surface for the general stroke cycle.

PIKE START

This is the fastest known start in competitive swimming. Like the 'hitch-kick' start, the take-off is at a slightly steeper angle than the grab start; the body appears to be straight but is still achieving height. In flight and at the apex of the parabola, the 'piking' of the body is created by the head and arm movements.

The main advantage of the pike dive is that it acquires greater height and distance off the block; this ensures that the weight of the body achieves angular entry to the water in a trajectory of maximum efficiency and therefore minimal resistance, enabling an extremely fast transition into the stroke. Movements of the head and arms in take-off and flight are more aggressive than those associated with the grab start and are employed so as to gain maximum effect from the transfer of momentum to the body. Some swimmers maintain that if you swim 50s without a 'pike dive' start, you are bound to collect a pennant instead of a medal.

Stance

The stance for the pike start is similar to that required in the 'grab start'. It is important that the swimmer does not angle forwards excessively on the block; if he does, he will find it very difficult to achieve sufficient velocity.

Take-Off

A number of movements occur simultaneously in a well co-ordinated take-off. firstly the head snaps forwards looking to the opposite end of the pool. The knees dip abruptly so as to maximize thrust, and the weight is transferred from the flat of the foot to the ball of the foot.

The hands release their hold on the block, they are thrust forwards, and then stopped and made to extend downwards at an angle towards the water; these simultaneous actions transfer momentum to the body and cause it to move rapidly outwards. The knees straighten and the body is propelled powerfully forwards and upwards.

Flight

The body is launched out in a relatively high-angled semi-circular parabola. At the apex of its path, the body is straight and almost parallel to the surface of the water. The head moves rapidly downwards with the eyes looking at the surface of the water, and the arms then move back from the forward position; the combined influence of the head and arm movements adds momentum to the piking of the hips. The head moves in further, bringing the chin onto the chest with the eyes looking backwards and the back of the head tucked below the biceps. At this stage the arms, head and upper body are almost at right angles to the lower

Fig 32a   In the pike start, the toes grip the edge of the block and the hands touch the feet or the block between the feet, according to individual preference; the angle of the upper and lower leg is approximately 140 degrees.

Fig 32b   In take-off the head moves forwards with the hands leaving their purchase on the block and the upper leg straightening to bring the body forwards.

Fig 32c   The head continues to move aggressively forwards whilst the knees make a dipping movement to maximize thrust. The weight of the body is now transferred to the balls of the feet.

Fig 32d   At the peak of the flight the body is straight and almost parallel to the water; the arms are dropped abruptly to a downward angle so as to transfer momentum to the bodyweight.

Fig 32f   As the arms and head enter, both move upwards with some hip movement, and the legs come into line with the body.

Fig 32e   The head moves rapidly downwards tucking in under the biceps. This movement coupled with the previous downwards movement of the arm causes a mid-air piking of the body.

Fig 32g   Having come into line, the legs now follow into the 'hole' in the water created by the arms and upper body. The feet are pointed to create maximum streamlining on entry.

body, and the swimmer is committed to entry.

Entry

The entry sequence is the same as that of the grab start.

THE HITCH-KICK START ——————

The mechanical principles explained earlier in this chapter are the basis for the hitch-kick start. To reiterate, the body will rotate to a certain degree in reaction to the opposing forces of the leg thrust sending it upwards and the gravitational pull on the bodyweight downwards. Moreover the law of motion specifies that if a body-mass (in this case a swimmer) in flight creates a smaller circular area, the 'moment of inertia' around the transverse axis is nominal; this results in even faster rotation around the body's radius. The trajectory of the hitch-kick start is higher than that of the grab start, and in terms of efficiency is second only to that of the pike start.

Fig 33a   The hitch-kick start. The angle of the upper and lower leg is 140 degrees. The hands may grip the block one on top of the other according to individual preference.

Fig 33d   The trajectory is high, and the feet are tucked right up to the hips with the head and arms moving downwards; all these movements ensure optimum rotation – and therefore speed – of the body.

Fig 33b   The head and arms move forwards in unison.

Fig 33e   The legs start to straighten as the hands enter the water; the upper body is in a streamlined position.

Fig 33c   The weight is transferred to the balls of the feet. A powerful thrust by the legs takes the body outwards and in a vertical path.

Fig 33f   The legs come into line with the upper body as it enters the 'hole' in the water made by the head and arms. The feet should now be together with the toes pointed.

Stance

The stance sequence is similar to that of other starts.

Take-Off

The take-off sequence is similar to that in the pike start.

Flight

The body is launched out in a high-angled semi-circular path with the head moving rapidly downwards and the eyes looking at the surface of the water. The arms are now brought somewhat downwards, at the same time as the feet are tucked right up to the hips so that the soles face up towards the ceiling (hitch-kick). At the apex of the flight as the body begins to rotate downwards the chin is pressed onto the chest so the eyes look backwards and the back of the head is tucked beneath the biceps. The arms, head and upper body are straight, and at this stage in line with the upper legs; the legs are still bent at the knee.

Entry

As the fingertips touch the surface of the water, the knees straighten and the arms move forwards once again. This has a reverse piking effect on the hips, which helps the legs to straighten and come into line with the upper body.

The fingertips enter first, creating a 'hole' in the water through which the rest of the body may follow; after entry the head follows the path of the arms forwards and upwards, and the head and arm movements together help the back to arch and the body to achieve a path which is parallel to the surface of the water. Experience alone teaches co-ordination and speed in achieving this objective.

THE TRACK START ─────────

The track start is seldom used in higher levels of competitive swimming because the other starting techniques are more effective. However, where the swimmer's technique is not good enough to manage the other starts, the track start is an acceptable option. In track events it is used so the athlete can get into his stride quickly and efficiently with horizontal velocity (momentum which is parallel to the surface of the track). As regards swimming, however, starting sequences require unified explosive power in order to create both vertical and horizontal velocity, and the track start for a swimmer is not nearly so effective because the angle of take-off is less in comparison to other starting techniques, and this will adversely affect the momentum in the initial transitional stage of the stroke.

Stance

The swimmer is bent over with one foot at the front and the other near the rear of the block. The upper and lower legs are at an angle to each other of approximately 140 degrees. The toes of the leading foot grip the front edge of the block, with the hands holding the leading edge on either side of the toes.

Take-Off

The head snaps forwards, looking to the opposite end of the pool, at the same time as the hands release their hold on the block. The hands are thrust forwards and are then stopped and made to extend downwards at an angle towards the water. The weight of the body is transferred to the balls of the feet. These combined actions move the body outwards, and the knees now straighten, also

Fig 34a The track start. The feet are 'staggered' on the block, toes over the edge, hands gripping outside the feet.

Fig 34b The hands release and start to extend ahead; the back foot and head are raised in unison, thereby moving the body forwards.

Fig 34c The left leg now thrusts downwards, upwards and outwards. Notice that the legs act independently, and so the strength of take-off, so important for vertical and outward velocity, is minimized.

Fig 34d The apex of the body's parabola is lower because the take-off is less powerful. Angular movements of both the head and the arms now occur and prepare the body for entry.

Fig 34e The back of the head tucks in under the biceps and follows the hands into the water.

propelling the body forwards and out.

Flight

The body is launched in a semi-circular path at a fairly shallow angle. The head moves rapidly downwards until the chin is pressed on chest with the eyes looking backwards. The arms now move down a little so the biceps cradle the back of the head. At this stage the arms and head and the upper and lower bodies are almost straight in line.

Entry

As the fingertips touch the surface of the water, the arms move forwards once again in line with the upper body thus creating a 'hole' in the water through which the rest of the body may follow.

After entry the head follows the path of the arms forwards and upwards, and this helps the back to arch. Experience alone teaches co-ordination so that the body achieves, as quickly as possible, a path which is parallel to the surface of the water.

RELAY TAKE-OVER STARTS ———

There are two main types of start that can be used in relay races: the wind-up start, and the start where the swimmer on the starting block 'targets' the incoming swimmer. The wind-up start is used in a relay take-over situation with the swimmer on the block in an upright position; this gives him a commanding view of the incoming swimmer. When the latter reaches a specific distance into the wall – usually as his head passes the 'tee-mark' on the pool bottom – the swimmer on the block commences his wind-up start: this entails a circular forward rotation of both arms, a movement which he will stop suddenly at a downward angle. The forward momentum of the body is therefore boosted by the transfer of additional momentum from the energy that was built up in the arm swing.

Once committed there is no recall in this type of start: if the incoming swimmer slows down for one reason or another, the take-over will not be synchronized. The wind-up start could be considered a somewhat precarious method for the younger age-grouper, and a more reliable technique might be the take-over where the swimmer on the block 'targets' the incoming swimmer. In this, the arms are extended with the fingers 'targeting' and following in on the head of the incoming swimmer. It is extremely simple, adequate and safe at all levels of age group swimming.

In any relay the first swimmer is the only one to use a normal starting technique; all other members of the relay squad would use a take-over technique in which they stand upright, either the 'wind-up' or the 'targeting' start.

THE WIND-UP TAKE-OVER START ——

Stance

The swimmer stands upright on the block, toes over and gripping the edge, with the eyes fixed on the incoming swimmer. Both arms are extended and pointing down, targeting on the head of the incoming swimmer.

Take-Off

The legs bend gradually as the hands are brought backwards to the legs; both heels are raised slightly, and the bodyweight transferred to the balls of the feet. The legs straighten, then dip again, with the weight once more transferred to the soles of the feet. This movement is co-ordinated to that of the head dropping and the arms swinging back. As the arms swing forwards again, the weight is once more transferred to the balls of the feet and the

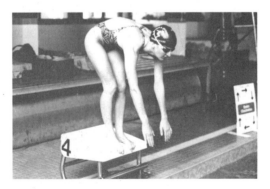

Fig 35a The wind-up start. The swimmer is upright and 'marking' the incoming swimmer.

Fig 35b   The hands/arms are swung back to the knees in the initial movement.

Fig 35f   The arms swing forwards and suddenly stop. The transfer of momentum brings the body forwards with the weight transferred to the balls of the feet.

Fig 35c   The legs straighten as the wind-up commences.

Fig 35g   The body is now in a position of flight.

Fig 35d   The knees start to bend and dip in synchronized movement with the arm swing.

Fig 35h   On the downward path the body is stretched and streamlined ready for entry.

Fig 35e   The arm swing continues backwards with the knees continuing to bend.

Fig 35i   The legs straighten in line with the toes pointing upwards.

whole body moves forwards, at the same time as the legs thrust off vigorously. The head suddenly lifts and targets into space. The arms are made to stop abruptly in mid-swing so for a moment they remain extended downwards, and the build-up of momentum is transferred to the body as it starts in flight.

Flight

The flight sequence is similar to that of the 'pike start'.

Entry

The entry sequence is similar to that of the 'pike start'.

Transition into the Stroke

The stroke determines the depth of entry. A shallower entry and shorter glide may be used for front crawl, and a greater depth and longer underwater phase for both butterfly and breaststroke.

THE TARGETING TAKE-OVER START–

Stance

This is similar to the stance in the wind-up start.

Take-Off

As the incoming swimmer approaches, the knees bend gradually, with the weight of the body on the soles of the feet. The back is rounded as the knees continue to bend until they reach an approximate angle of 140 degrees. As the incoming swimmer touches the wall, Both hands 'strike' the front edge of the block and push strongly away from it, and are then thrust forwards. As the head

lifts and targets into space the body moves forwards. The weight is transferred to the balls of the feet as the legs dip and straighten vigorously. The downward extending hands are stopped

Fig 36a   The targeting stance. The swimmer on the block is upright, targeting his hands on the incoming

Fig 36b   The knees bend, the rate at which they do so synchronizing with the speed of the incoming swimmer's approach.

Fig 36c   The knees continue to bend as the swimmer in the water approaches with undiminished speed, central in the lane and finishing under the middle of the starting block.

Fig 36d   The incoming swimmer takes a last breath of oxygen as he sights the 'tee' on the pool bottom, enabling him to make a smooth, fast finish into the wall.

Fig 36e   As the swimmer in the water hits the wall with the leading hand, the swimmer above strikes the block thus gaining impetus into the initial starting sequence.

Fig 36f   The head and arms lift outwards and upwards with the legs thrusting powerfully against the block.

abruptly in mid-swing and the body takes off in flight.

Flight

The flight sequence is similar to that of the 'pike start' in that the body is launched out in a relatively high-angled, semi-circular path. The head is very quickly tipped downwards, with the eyes looking at the surface of the water. Both arms now move back from the forward position; this action, combined with the head movement, adds momentum to the piking of the hips. At this phase of the start the body is straight and almost parallel to the surface of the water. The chin now moves onto the chest with the eyes looking backwards and the biceps passing close over the back of the head. At this precise moment the arms, head and upper body are straight and in line, with the lower body almost at right angles. The body is now committed to the downward phase of the flight path.

Entry

The entry is similar to that of previous starts.

Transition into the Stroke

Each stroke determines the depth of entry. A shallower entry and shorter glide may be used for front crawl, with a greater depth and longer underwater phase for both butterfly and breaststroke.

BACK CRAWL START

Age-group swimmers usually have difficulty in achieving the degree of trajectory necessary for this start. Everything depends on the angles of the levers in the stance position. It is important that the toes are only just under the surface of the water; if they are any lower the water level will cover the hips, and this will create resistance for an outward and then upward movement. The hands should grip the rail on the blocks at shoulder-width apart.

Opinion differs concerning the best position for the feet on the wall: some coaches favour the feet being together, others for one foot lower than the other. One argument for this latter technique is that if one foot slips, the other can still function for the drive away from the wall; another is that if both feet are in line when the drive off the wall takes place, the stronger foot will launch the swimmer in a path of curvature (to one side or the other) away from the wall. Nevertheless, the propulsive effect of both feet in line will undoubtedly be greater than the 'staggered' placement of the feet (unity is strength).

No matter where the feet are placed, it is vitally important that an energetic head movement occurs before the leg drive: the swimmer should always 'go' to the head in the first initial action. If this does not happen the feet will slip, because if the legs seek any sort of initial drive against the wall in the take-off, the outcome of the direction of force will be downward. However, if the head is thrown backwards first, followed by the arms and upper body, then the impetus resulting from the leg drive will be upward and backward. A common fault is to achieve minimal movement of the head, with the result that the application of force is backwards, against the pressure of water.

There is another difference of opinion concerning the position of the arms during the take-off. If the arms recover overhead (following a path of the body line), then the body will achieve good depth on entry. But if the arms are thrown to the side, the latter part of the movement creates a 'scything', broader entry on the water. The depth can be therefore be controlled according to the type of arm entry employed. Every swimmer should experiment with both techniques to find which action suits him best.

Stance

If at 'take-off' the arms are to follow a path along the body line, then the hands should grasp the rail of the starting block shoulder-width apart. If the arms are to be thrown to the side, then the hands should grasp the rail on the grips to the side of the block. The head looks down towards the feet; the back follows the natural curvature of the spine governed by the position of the head. The arms are equally bent at the elbows. The toes must be just under the surface of the water. Both feet are placed on the wall (to suit the individual) with the weight of the body balanced on the toes. The legs are bent at the knees (with the chin almost touching), with the upper leg at approximately 140 degrees to the lower leg, and the seat of the swimmer 'sitting' on the surface of the water.

Take-Off

The head is propelled backwards vigorously, facing upwards, then backwards, but with a continuity of movement which continues well into flight. Both arms may be thrown – almost in unison with the head movement – either backwards or to the side. When the upper body is at an approximate angle of 40 degrees to the surface of the water, the legs straighten forcefully and the body is projected upwards and backwards.

Fig 37a   The hands hold the starting block at the side grips with the eyes looking down at the feet. The seat of the swimmer is at, or just under, the surface of the water.

Fig 37d   Only now does the swimmer go to the legs, allowing them to straighten and thrust him powerfully upwards and backwards.

Fig 37b   At the starting signal the head is thrown back to its extremity as the hands release their hold on the block.

Fig 37e   The arms catch up and pass the head, then continue in a path downwards. This causes the back to arch so the hands can enter first.

Fig 37c   The body continues backwards from the initial movement of the upper trunk and head.

Fig 37f   The rest of the body follows the entry path of the hands with the legs being the final component to enter.

Flight

The head continues to move backwards until the eyes are facing the far end of the pool with the the the back of the head lower than the shoulder width of the swimmer. The back is arched into extension as the arms catch up and pass the head before coming in on an inward path.

Entry

The fingertips enter first, with the hands still striving to come together. These are followed by the back of the head, the shoulders, and the arched shape of the body curving into the area of entry. The hands come together and position themselves one on top of the other, with the head tucked between the biceps; this achieves an efficient, streamlined body position.

Transition into the Stroke

Both head and arms are adjusted to the depth most suitable for the glide and leg action. According to the rules concerning start and turn procedures the swimmer can be completely submerged for a distance of not more than 15 metres; by this point the head must have broken the surface of the water. The number of underwater kicking cycles this involves is up to the individual swimmer, and generally depends on the event in question and the efficiency of the leg action. Normally a relative number of leg cycles takes place as the velocity of the glide diminishes to swimming speed. Lifting the head together with a strong arm action will bring the body to the surface of the water where one arm recovers as the other arm breaks into full stroke.

THE TEACHING AND COACHING OF STARTS AND TAKE-OVERS

The basic techniques of the 'plunge dive' should have been mastered at teaching levels. The 'grab start' is the easier start for the swimmer to master in progressive steps of teaching and coaching. A group of swimmers must learn each phase one step at a time, and there are six phases for each start taking it from when the swimmer first ascends the block. Little improvement in technique will be made if the swimmer is taken through the entire sequence in one action.

The swimmers should be in groups behind each of the blocks, with one swimmer ascending the block and implementing just one point of technique, then changing places with the next swimmer in line. The variety of starting techniques that are considered in this chapter have a similarity in some of the phases. Each technique must be studied in depth in order to achieve success; the related practices will enhance each different technique.

In the 'take-over' practices, have at least four swimmers to each block. The first swimmer goes in on a normal start and takes two arm-strokes; he makes a 360-degree somersault (additional turn practice), turns toward the block, takes in oxygen and comes in for the take-over. This practice re-establishes orientation, makes the swimmer look for the wall, and is also the correct distance out to take in the last breath of oxygen before 'take-over'.

Coaching Practices for the Grab Start

Coaching Phases	*Coaching Practices/Points*
Up on the blocks	1. Stand comfortably on the block 2. Bend over 3. Arms hang loose 4. Eyes look straight down 5. Legs are straight
Take your marks (stance position)	1. With 2 step forwards, curl the toes over the lip of the block 2. Feet in line with the hips 3. Legs at 140 degree angle 4. Grab the block either side of/between/hand on hand on/the feet 5. Thumbs assisting the fingers 6. Head downward and backward
Take-off: phase 1	1. On the command 'up', the arms are thrust outwards to reach an inclined angle downwards to the water 2. The upper trunk alone moves upwards with the swimmer holding the 140 degree angle of the legs 3. The head snaps up to pillow between arms; eyes looking for the tops of the fingers 4. Hold the position until told to step down
Take-off: phase 2	1. 'This time you are going' 2. Bring the weight forwards onto toes 3. Don't go to the legs early 4. Snap the head and arms upwards 5. Legs straighten and thrust vigorously backwards on the block
Flight	1. Head and arms move downwards for entry 2. Pillow the head between the arms
Entry	1. Hand to go on top of hand for streamlined entry 2. As the fingertips enter, the arms and head go forwards; arch the back 3. Keep legs stretched and toes pointed
Stroke transition	1. Short glide in a maximized streamlined position followed by stroke sequences. In front crawl sequence 4/6 kicking cycles followed by a vigorous arm action 2. Head raises as arm action commences 3. Hold the stroke cycle briefly then commence

Coaching Practices for the Pike Dive

Coaching Phases	*Coaching Practices/Points*
Up on the blocks	Similar to the grab start
Take your marks (stance position)	Similar to the grab start
Take-off	Initial practices as in grab start take-off phase 1. Then diving over a rope across the pool, first at knee height then adjust higher for distance and velocity. Also diving into a teaching hoop 1. Head snaps forwards looking to the endof the pool 2. Arms thrust upwards/forwards and stop, hands inclined towards water surface 3. Dip the knees then go onto toes 4. Forceful leg action 5. Powerful take-off outwards and upwards
Flight	1. Two synchronized movements of the head and arms as they move downwards: chin to chest, and the back of the head is tucked between the biceps
Entry and stroke transition	Similar to the grab start

Coaching Practices for Take-Overs

The Wind-up Take-over

Coaching Phases	Coaching Practices/Points
Stance	1. Swimmer stands upright; toes gripping edge; eyes fixed on incoming swimmer 2. Arms extended downwards and targeting the approaching swimmer
Take-off	1. Legs gradually bend and arms brought back to knees 2. A rocking movement occurs which is synchronized with the head dropping and a swinging arm movement 3. Arms swing forwards and weight transferred again to toes 4. Vigorous leg drive with head lifting 5. Movement of arms suddenly stopped at a down ward angle in mid-swing
Flight and entry	Similar to sequences of the grab start
Transition and take-over	1. Don't breathe into the stroke 2. Take 2 stroke cycles (arms) 3. Full somersault 4. Take in oxygen 5. Swim in over the black line 6. Don't breathe on the way in

The Targeting Take-over

Coaching Phases	*Coaching Practices/Points*
Stance	1. Swimmer stands upright; toes gripping edge; eyes fixed on the incoming swimmer
Take-off	1. Arms extended downwards and targeting the approaching swimmer: 'Mark the incoming swimmer' 2. Legs gradually bend like a coiling spring; back rounded; toes gripping the edge of the block; as incoming swimmer touches, the hands strike and thrust forwards away from the block; weight goes on toes and legs straighten explosively; head lifts, targets on pool end and the arms are stopped (downward angle)
Flight and entry	Similar sequence to pike or grab starts
Transisition and take-over	Similar sequence, practices and coaching points to the wind-up take-over

Coaching Practices for the Backstroke Start

Coaching Phases	*Coaching Practices/Points*
Stance	1. Hands on grips shoulder-width apart 2. Head looks down to feet 3. Arms bent at elbows; equal angles of lower and upper arms 4. Toes just covered by water level 5. Legs bent at the knees with chin almost touching knees 6. Upper leg 140 degrees to lower leg 7. Seat of swimmer 'sits' on water surface
Take-off	To show how much head movement there is, the swimmer should first be in a crouched position (standing on pool bottom), hands on the side or scum trough, the head should move backwards until the swimmer can see the water level at the far end of the pool 1. Head must move first and is forcefully thrown back

Coaching Phases	*Coaching Practices/Points*
	2. The arms are thrown backwards (or sideways) in unison with the head movement 3. The legs straighten powerfully, taking the body upward and outward Note: Coaching practice: hold the grips and move the head back so far that the swimmer can see the other end of the pool. Wearing a shirt (to protect the back), practise starts from the pool steps (logical height)
Flight	1. Head and arms thrown backwards 2. Head to be lower than the shoulder line 3. Back to be arched 4. Arms thrown to the side for shallow entry; down body line for depth
Entry	1. Hand on top of hand 2. Head pillowed between biceps
Transition into stroke	1. Hold glide until swimming speed (trial and error) is reached 2. Adjust leg action cycles to individual preference; too many and oxygen debt will result. Dolphin or alternating sequence 3. Lifting of the head and strong arm action for surface stroking

7

Competitive Turns

A turn in competitive swimming is a means of changing direction at the end of each length as quickly and efficiently as possible. The basic mechanical principles discussed and applied to starting techniques in Chapter 5 are also applicable to turning techniques. Momentum can be described as either linear or angular; with reference to turns, in the front crawl tumble turn and the back crawl flip turn for example, there is a transfer of forward (linear) motion into angular motion. In this instance, the moment of inertia is small about the transverse axis because the swimmer tucks into the shape of a ball. In the breaststroke, butterfly, the individual medley turns (except for the back flip) and throw-away turns, the extended shape of the swimmer on approaching and leaving the wall creates a moment of inertia that is large about the transverse axis, and linear motion is to a large extent compromised because the swimmer touches the wall. Thus the circular-shaped form of a swimmer will turn faster than that of an extended shape. However, this is only true for a proportion of the turn because if the legs can generate forceful acceleration out of the turning movement, the turn can be even faster. And if other applications of the levers are added to the turning momentum, then the turn becomes faster

still. To analyse this precept further, the leg action in front crawl applies force in the downward movement; how powerful this might be is in proportion to the contraction of the muscle groups and the area of the lever. The combined leg action of butterfly is even more effective, so if, at the commencement of the front crawl turn, the leg action changes from an alternating pattern to a dolphin kick down, it will be very much more effective. This is because the surface area of both legs pushes against a relatively greater area of water, using it as a 'springboard' for momentum into fast rotation.

There have been many innovations over the last two decades: the butterfly 'pullout' in the underwater phase of the breaststroke turn revolutionized it. In front crawl the arms 'pulling up' coupled with the dolphin kick down gave rotational speed. Even the individual medley saw changes, with a 'spin-over' onto the breast position in the back-to-breast leg. But the greatest change must be the flip turn in the back crawl event, the result of an alteration in the FINA laws; this led to greater speeds being achieved, while the techniques of the turn and the related teaching and coaching methods were much simpler altogether.

The whole point of rule changes is to promote faster swimming. If swimming in general is to progress, then such changes should continue to be made. A case in point might be teaching and coaching practices which are designed to conform with natural water principles but where there is often a conflict between these principles and man-made laws; a prime example of this is the re-active sequence in the underwater phase of the breaststroke turn (see below, the breaststroke turn sequence). The impetus for change generally comes from outside FINA; for instance, in the World Cup series, a great many people lobbied for the rule change in the back crawl turn. Also, a national governing body can sug-gest that a rule change is considered by the FINA National Technical Committee. Faults usually come to the fore in the early days of implementation, and the rule governing the back crawl turn (1991) was no exception to these early teething problems.

The various stages of any turn may be identified as follows: approach; plant; turn; push off; and transition into stroke.

THE FRONT CRAWL TURN ————————

There are three types of turn associated with this stroke:

1. The throw-away turn
2. The tumble turn
3. The flip turn

THE THROW-AWAY TURN ————————

This turn is used by many swimmers, and the basic concepts of it are applied exten-sively by social swimmers everywhere. The more advanced version is used by many people competitively, such as in 'Masters' events and by club swimmers who use it in shallow-depth pools (also when the coach isn't looking). It is excel-lent for use by any competitive swimmer who may have a temporary back problem where a tumble turn would normally exacerbate the trouble, and executed properly it is only marginally slower than the tumble turn in an average type of competition.

The various degrees of 'eddy current' and profile resistance, have already been discussed (Chapter 1), but the principles are especially relevant here. So, when turning after the 'approach' and 'plant' sequences, a swimmer may rotate 180 degrees and present the front of the body to the drive off the wall. However, this creates eddy currents and certainly pro-file resistance, and in order to minimize these effects the sectional area of body must be reduced. If the swimmer reduces the amount he rotates to 90 degrees, the side of the body only is presented to the water in the drive off the wall. This reduces the body area and movement and therefore the resistance factors, and the swimmer will 'knife' away from the wall into the water much more quickly.

It is important to realize that if the head turns more than 90 degrees, the upper trunk must also rotate in move-ment; even in the initial stages of the turn when the turning head comes to face the wall the trunk rotates minimally. For the body to 'knife' into the water, the upper trunk movement and therefore the head as the controlling factor must be strictly limited.

Movement of the head is the main problem for the younger age-grouper, and it must be rigidly controlled in any turn associated with this technique. It is essential that the eyes fix on the touching hand in the movement away from the wall, with the hand then following a path over the head and central body line. If the hand is thrown, it may come out of alignment and drag the body round.

The necessary depth is created by three actions: the side of the body 'knifing' into the water with a minimum of resistance; the trailing hand pulling palm upwards against the water; and the 'javelin' effect of the hand as it slices centrally into the water with the thumb and forefinger leading. The throw-away turn is good in its own right; as a constructive drill for breaststroke, butterfly and certain sequences in the individual medley, it is excellent.

Approach

One hand reaches for the wall whilst the other trails by the hip. A deep breath of

Fig 38a   The leading hand reaches for the wall with the other trailing; the body is completely on its side.

Fig 38b   The fingertips touch first followed by the palm of the hand; the elbows flex progressively: all these movements synchronize perfectly with the incoming speed. The head comes in close to the wall, with the eyes locked to a point above the touching hand.

Fig 38d   The eyes remain fixed on the hand as it 'slices' away from the wall, tracing a linear path over the centre line of the body.

Fig 38c   With the eyes, and so also the head, fixed rigidly on the leading hand, the body and arm move rapidly away from the wall. The feet are in the 'crucifix' position as they meet with the wall, and the body moves like a pendulum throughout this phase.

Fig 38e   The hand now 'javelins' into the water ahead of the body, a movement that, together with the trailing arm pulling upwards, achieves the necessary depth away from the wall.

oxygen is taken just before contact with the wall. The kicking sequence is completed, bringing the body into the wall with undiminished speed; it moves from an 'on breast' position onto its side.

Plant

The fingers touch first, followed by the palm of the hand with the fingertips pointing upwards. The elbow bends in relation to the speed of the approach, and continues to flex until the head is close to the wall. Under the water the knees bend and the feet come together, the instep of one foot tucking into the sole of the other; this is known as the crucifix position, and it minimizes resistance. The body is upright with the eyes fixed rigidly on the touching hand.

Turn and Push-Off

A co-ordinated movement takes place between the upper body and the arm as they move and push vigorously away from the wall; the upper body falls away from the wall with the back of the head leading. The trailing hand pulls upwards against the pressure of water, with the touching hand leaving the wall thumb downwards; the eyes follow the initial movement of the touching hand as it traces a straight path over the head and then 'javelins' deep into the water. In a co-ordinated movement, once the hands have left the feet are planted momentarily on the wall, then push forcefully away with the body still on its side and the arms uniting together in a streamlined movement.

Transition into Stroke (Front Crawl)

The body 'spirals' onto the breast as the legs followed by the arms (led by the

lower arm) go into their stroke cycle. Oxygen is taken after the second arm cycle has been completed.

THE TUMBLE TURN

The tumble turn consists of a half-somersault (when forward linear motion changes to angular motion), then a half-twist out of the somersault, helped by the hands sculling in a reactive pattern. The body is now 'side-on' to the wall and the swimmer is ready for 'push-off'. This all sounds simple, although the younger age-grouper or the uninitiated swimmer would probably not agree when the theory is put into practice. The tumble turn is a swimmer's first introduction to controlled breathing and levels of oxygen debt, and at an early age the prospect of going without oxygen for anything up to three or four seconds is daunting to say the least. The technique becomes even harder in a 50m pool complex; nonetheless swimmers must always be encouraged to tumble at each end of the pool.

Exhalation takes place during the full underwater turning technique; in the early stages, young swimmers must be told to breathe out through the nostrils in order to equalize the pressure of water as they somersault over. It may take anything up to six months or a year before satisfactory turning standards are reached, and during this period only regular practices under the supervision of a coach will achieve perfection, as with any turning technique.

Approach

The tumble turn starts with a fast approach into the wall; as one hand finishes the propulsive phase it is stopped at the hip and turned palm downwards. As the

Coaching Practices for the Throw-Away Turn

Coaching Phases	*Coaching Practices/Points*
Approach	Swim in, touch the wall (1 hand touching, 1 arm trailing)
Plant	1. Elbow bends bringing the head close to the wall, eyes on touching hand 2. Body is on its side 3. Legs bend at knees with knees brought up towards midriff; feet in the 'crucifix' position
Turn	1. Body moves like a pendulum; head moves away from the wall and arm straightens 2. As hand leaves the wall the feet contact the wall 3. 'Fall back': the back of the head strikes the water, with the hand tracing a linear arc over the head 4. Hand (side on) 'javelins' into the water; it must *not* be thrown with any force
Push-off	1. Hand goes on top of hand for maximum streamlining 2. Head goes to the 'biceps tucked in' position 3. Legs now straighten powerfully, then tuck one behind the other helping to bring the body on breast with a rudder-like action
Transition into stroke	1. Leg action starts as speed from wall lessens 2. Lower arm starts to pull, with head turning centrally 3. After 1–2 arm cycles breathing cycle takes place

The Throw-Away Turn Sequence

Fig 39a The swimmer approaches the wall with the right hand, having finished the propulsive phase, staying in the region of the hip; it must now turn palm down.

Fig 39d The hands also contribute to the rotation of the turn by pulling up vigorously towards the head. The body is now in the position of a half-somersault.

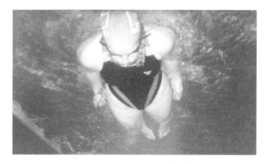

Fig 39b Both hands are now turned palm down and the leg action changes from an alternating pattern to a dolphin kick down, the legs coming together and flexing at the knees.

Fig 39e After the dolphin kick down, the legs accelerate forcefully out of the water and are thrown at the wall; the hands continue to pull upwards.

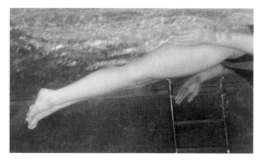

Fig 39c The legs now synchronize in a dolphin kick downwards; this action drives the hips upwards, thus contributing greatly to the rotational aspect of the turn.

Fig 39f Both hands now press sideways against the water, and this action – with a minimum movement from the hip region – causes the body to turn out of the half-somersault and into the half-twist, and so onto its side.

Fig 39g   As the feet hit the wall the body is completely on its side. The incoming speed of the swimmer is still considerable and when the toes, followed by the soles of the feet, connect with the wall, the knees bend even more; these three movements are synchronized with the speed of the approach. The body is now coiled like a spring for acceleration away from the wall.

Fig 39i   The body rotates back onto the breast position, an action which is assisted by one foot moving behind the other, then coming vigorously into the other foot in a 'rudder-like' action.

Fig 39j   The swimmer is now completely on breast and commences the normal cycle of stroke.

Fig 39h   As the swimmer accelerates away from the wall, the arms are fully extended. One hand locks on top of the other, with the head pillowed into and beneath the biceps.

forward arm completes its outward and inward scull, it, too, is moved onto the hip and turned palm downwards. Two movements then occur simultaneously which promote an impressive amount of rotational speed: the chin dips onto the chest, and the leg action changes from an alternating pattern to a single dolphin kick down which drives the hips up.

The upper portion of the body rotates quickly, and the arms now pull upwards towards the head; the arm movement is fractionally behind that of the head movement and the dolphin kick down.

At this moment the upper body is at right angles to the legs, with the body in the position of a half-somersault. By kicking strongly against the water the legs can accelerate powerfully out of the water towards the wall.

Fractionally before the feet hit the wall, the hands turn to face palm outwards and push against the water. This action, combined with the head turning and a minimal movement from the hips, causes the body to start moving into the half-twist.

Plant

The balls of the feet are planted on the wall with the knees bending at right angles and the body continuing to twist until it is side-on to the wall. Having completed the sideways sculling action, the hands now start to extend ahead.

Push-off

The knees straighten powerfully; the arms are now fully extended (hand on hand) in a position of maximum streamlining. Both feet are tucked into each other with the upper foot behind the lower, thus giving better longitudinal rotation. The head is tucked in between the arms as the body continues to twist onto the full breast position.

Transition into the Stroke

The upper leg bends at the knee and then drives down for the commencement of the kicking cycle. If the arm action takes place while the body is still at an angle, then the lower arm will commence the first arm cycle. Usually four to six kicks will take place, followed by one complete arm cycle before the swimmer takes in oxygen.

Teaching the Tumble Turn

The turn can be taught with up to eight swimmers in each lane at the shallow end of the pool. The swimmers are numbered off, with ones on the right of the lane and twos on the left, and lined up behind one another with a good gap in between. The first practice is a tuck somersault (where they stand), and the teaching point should be to keep the head central and the shoulders parallel to the surface of the water as they go over. In order to show the effect of dragging water, in the next practice they should place the chin on their dipped shoulder as they go over; the outcome of this exercise is bodies facing

in all different directions when they come up, and demonstrates how important it is for the shoulders always to be square as they go over. To avoid the risk of the young age-grouper hitting his head on the wall, he should somersault well away from it.

A good target point for the more proficient is to 'brush' the fingers of the touching hand down the wall as the somersault commences. As practice improves technique, this targeting factor will not be required (it takes about six months to establish proficiency in the turn).

Swimmers may now attempt the turn properly, with two in each lane swimming in, then tumbling at the wall. As they come out of the turn and swim down the centre of the lane they somersault again at the end of the queue. The arms establish the half-twist in the turn by sculling sideways underwater, although this must not be taught as it will lead to confusion. The sculling action will occur naturally; the problem at this point is gaining full extension of the arms off the wall. The arms should start to extend as soon as the rotational aspect of the turn commences; an exercise to practise this is for the swimmers to stand up and extend the arms straight above the head with the hands together at extension. The teaching point would be that you require 'fast arm movement as the turn commences'.

A practice which follows on from the arm extending exercise is to achieve a dolphin leg action as the somersault commences. Further practices with more competent swimmers might include the feet coming out of the water fast; then to straighten the legs and 'throw' them over the water with a 'crack-down' on the surface of the water (known as 'crack-overs'). Finally they might try an exercise to practise finishing the arm action at the hips with the palms facing down, then

Coaching Practices for the Tumble Turn

Coaching Phases	*Coaching Practices/Points*
Approach	1. The swimmer approaches the wall at speed 2. As one arm is halfway through its cycle it is stopped at the hip and then turned palm downward; the other arm then does the same so both hands are now palm down 3. Chin goes on the chest 4. The alternating leg action changes to a dolphin movement downward, driving the hips up; both legs drive up out of the water and are thrown at the wall 5. The hands bend at the elbow pulling up towards the head (this helps the rotational movement of the body) 6. Halfway through the forward somersault a half-twist develops, due to the hands sculling sideways under the water, aided by a hip movement
Plant	Balls of the feet strike the wall with a nominal amount of knee bend
Turn	1. The legs bend at the knee still more 2. The body, already side-on, is now ready to leave the wall 3. The arms complete their extension ahead with one hand on top of the other
Push-off	1. The legs push away vigorously from the all 2. Head pillowed between the biceps
Transition into stroke	1. Leg action starts as speed from the wall lessens 2. Lower arm starts to pull with head turning centrally 3. After 1–2 arm cycles, breathing cycle takes place

Front Crawl Flip Turn Sequence

Fig 40a   The swimmer approaches the wall with the final stroke being taken by the left arm.

Fig 40d   The legs somersault from the water and are thrown through the air at the wall. The hands continue to pull upwards, then start to extend ahead.

Fig 40b   Both hand stop at the hips, and the alternating leg action changes to a single dolphin kick down.

Fig 40e   As the feet make contact with the wall the arms are at full extension. The legs push away from the wall vigorously, and the swimmer extends away from the wall on his back.

Fig 40c   Midway through the dolphin kick the hands start to pull upwards towards the head.

Fig 40f   Coupled with head movement and a rudder-like movement of the feet, the swimmer spirals back onto the breast position, then kicks and pulls into the full stroke cycle.

pulling the arms upwards towards the head as the somersault commences.

THE FRONT CRAWL FLIP TURN ——

Unlike the front crawl tumble turn where the half-twist comes in midway through the half-somersault, in the flip turn the two actions are quite separate. The swimmer flips onto the back, pushes off and then half twists after leaving the wall. All the actions which facilitated the rotational aspects of the tumble turn are used in the flip turn; also the longitudinal (rotational) aspects of the half twist which bring the body back to the breast position after leaving the wall are similar.

The flip turn is a far easier turn to coach with the young age group swimmer, and if it is used as a progressive practice it will establish a more proficient tumble turn in the early stages. Thus when attempting the tumble turn in early practices, young swimmers 'stay on the wall' and twist onto the 'on breast' position; if they are told to half twist after leaving the wall, this twisting action is completed early and leads to a prominent tumble turn.

Which is Faster?

Some time ago as coach at the Chelsea and Kensington Club, I did an assessment and breakdown of timed turns. The first set showed a small percentage gain of the flip turn over the tumble. The second set showed a marked increase in time gained but as the experiment continued the totals became lower on the flip turn in relation to the tumble. A general conclusion might be drawn that whatever we decide upon in swimming we should always bear in mind that one type of technique may suit one swimmer and

another type will suit someone else. Obviously the flip turn technique suited this particular swimmer, but it may not suit another individual.

Teaching the Flip Turn

The flip turn is much easier to teach than the tumble turn. The swimmers should be organized in a similar way to the tumble-turn practices, and somersaults should be practised first, with a swim into the wall and a half-somersault to bring the swimmer off the wall on his back; the teaching point should be that the head must look up to the ceiling. Next, the swimmer might push off from the wall, cross the feet one behind the other and half-twist onto the breast position. The complete flip turn is very easy to teach – simply duplicate the initial practices from the tumble turn; and it is obviously easily learned because progress is made quickly.

THE BACK CRAWL FLIP TURN ——

The most satisfying amendment to FINA laws resulted in changes to the back crawl turn. Difficulties were always encountered when teaching the previous turn, particularly as it suffered from many different interpretations and titles, the most common being the 'spin turn'. A faster edition was the 'head up' or Naber turn, used extensively in the seventies; age-groupers tended to use this turn right up until 1991 when the 'flip' turn came onto the scene. In international competition the 'crossover' (sometimes called the 'suicide turn') was the preferred technique among the elite. It was first seen in Britain used by Phillip Hubble – and by other British swimmers who were residing at American universities – at various meets. However, as with many

The Back Crawl Flip Turn Sequence

Fig 41a   The swimmer approaches the wall.

Fig 41d   The right arm completes the downward phase and now turns so the palm faces backwards and assists the left arm in maintaining pressure on the water in order to keep up forward progression.

Fig 41b   The body now starts to roll over into the half-twist, assisted by the right arm which completes the stroke cycle and comes up to a high elbow position (above the water), then 'javelins' down into the water.

Fig 41e   The left arm having perfected its propulsive cycle now turns with the palm facing downwards.

Fig 41c   The right arm continues in a downward path, while the left arm maintains pressure on the water for forward speed.

Fig 41f The right hand continues 'fixing' on the water right through to the region of the hip. The alternating action of the legs continues until they are both in a downward position.

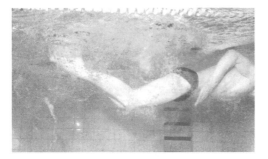

Fig 41g Both hands now at the hips start to turn palm upwards, at the same time as the legs are brought up to the surface and give a dolphin kick downwards. This achieves rotational speed of the hips and accelerates the initial action of the legs as they come out of the water before making contact with the wall.

Fig 41j Having made contact with the wall, the legs bend and then push powerfully away from the wall; the body is streamlined, with the hands and arms fully extended ahead of the swimmer.

Fig 41h The hands now pull upwards towards the head. This action, combined with the dolphin kick down, contributes significantly to faster rotation.

Fig 41k As velocity away from the wall diminishes and the swimmer reaches swimming speed, he uses a number of dolphin leg movements. The arms and head now angle up towards the surface.

Fig 41i The hands continue to pull upwards as the legs continue their path out of the half-somersault and now make contact with the wall.

Fig 41l One arm cycle with the head in a raised position brings the swimmer to the surface where the arms and legs resume the normal back crawl swimming sequence.

Coaching Practices for the Flip Turn

Coaching Phases	Coaching Practices/Points
Approach	1. The swimmer approaches the wall at speed 2. As one arm is over halfway through its cycle it stops at the hip and then turns palm downwards; the other arm does the same so both hands are now palm down 3. The chin is tucked onto the chest 4. The alternating leg action changes to a dolphin movement downwards, driving the hips up; both legs drive up out of the water and are thrown at the wall 5. The hands bend at the elbow, pulling up towards the head; this aids the rotational movement of the body 6. A forward somersault takes place with the feet being thrown at the wall
Plant	The feet strike the wall with a nominal bend which increases in relation to the incoming speed
Push-off	1. The legs push vigorously away from the wall 2. The head is pillowed between the biceps 3. The body is supine with the head looking up to the ceiling
Transition into stroke	1. The feet tuck in one behind another 2. The head starts to turn downwards 3. As the body rotates onto the breast position, the leg action commences as speed from the wall lessens 4. The lower arm starts to pull with the head turning centrally 5. After 1–2 arm cycles the breathing cycle takes place

innovations it was initially viewed with suspicion by officialdom, and disqualifications were widespread until it was accepted as the norm. Changes to FINA law then brought in the technique as we know it today; initially it, too, met with suspicion, and the different interpretations led to further amendments and clarifications in order to clear up the controversy that surrounded it. Again time has turned full circle, and the turn has become accepted by all.

Considered in simple terms, the back crawl flip turn is a half-twist into a half somersault –in other words, a reversal in technique to the front crawl flip turn. It is very much easier to teach than the old 'spin' turn, largely because of its linear type of rotational movement as compared to the circular sideways movement of the older turn. Amongst the turn's many attributes are the faster times which have resulted in the stroke.

More experienced swimmers will turn about two metres from the wall, younger age-groupers will turn closer. Once the swimmer half-twists onto the breast position, all the techniques of the front crawl flip turn can be used as long as the movements are continuous: dolphin kick down, fast leg movement out of the water and onto the wall, the arms pulling up towards the head. The rotational aspect of the turn is greatly improved if the final arm movement going into the somersault is with the elbow higher than the hand, and the speed of entry and depth is vigorous – that is, the hand should be near the head at entry. However, the hands now have to work exceptionally quickly to scull upwards so as to add to the rotational forces. This one factor and the relative sculling pattern is the latest improvement to have been made with the turn.

Approach

At the second to last arm action from the turning flags the head and body begin a synchronized sideways turning movement: the body starts to roll over into a half-twist, a rotational movement assisted by the opposite arm entering near the head and spearing downwards, then sculling up to aid rotation further. Both arm actions provoke the initial movement of the half-somersault, and this is further enhanced by a dolphin movement of the legs in their drive downwards. The legs are then thrown over the water as the arms start to extend ahead.

Plant

The balls of the feet strike the wall, followed by the soles of the feet, and the legs bend increasingly relative to the speed and force with which they hit the wall. The arms gain full extension with one hand on the top of the other and the head tucking in between the biceps.

Push-off

As the bodyweight transfers from the sole to the ball of the feet, the legs straighten and push vigorously away from the wall, with the body quickly assuming an efficient and streamlined position.

Transition into the Stroke

The swimmer describes a number of dolphin-like movements before commencing an arm cycle. The arm movement, together with the head being raised, brings the body back to the surface where the alternating movement of both arms and legs resumes.

Practices for the Back Crawl Flip Turn

1. Swimmers should line up one behind the other in shallow water lanes behind the turning flags.
2. To start with they swim in and count the number of pulls (half-cycles) before they touch the wall.
3. Then swim in and count the number of pulls minus two, then half-twist onto the breast position.
4. Swimmers might next practise forward tuck somersaults followed by dolphin kicks down and 'crack-overs'.
5. Swim in, half-twist then somersault with the feet meeting the wall. Swim down the lane to the end of the line of swimmers and perform another 'crack-over' (somersault with fast feet).
6. In this exercise swimmers push off from the wall on the back in a streamlined position, hand on hand. Half-twist onto the breast, then swim down the line and do another 'crack-over'.
7. Swim in at speed to practise the full flip turn. Off the wall half-twist onto the front, and at the end of the line a 'crack-over' again.

THE BREASTSTROKE AND BUTTERFLY TURNS ──────────

There are many similarities between breaststroke and butterfly turns; in fact the approach, plant, turn and push-off are exactly the same in both, and the main difference is that the butterfly turn is far less involved in the path away from the wall. In the butterfly transition to stroke, a dolphin kicking movement takes place with an under-water cycle and then a recovery above the surface of the water. Certain phases are used and are similar to both strokes, so if the techniques in the breaststroke turn are mastered then the butterfly techniques will follow accordingly.

At a clinic at Crystal Palace (London) in 1978, Doc Counsilman introduced me and several others to the then more recent innovations concerning the breaststroke turn. The butterfly underwater pulling pattern did more for the breaststroke start and turn sequence in Britain than any other had achieved before; the new techniques became standard practice within weeks throughout the UK, giving greater distance away from the block and the wall.

The breaststroke start and turn technique is the most complex and intriguing of all. The turn can be broken down into two main components, one involving the approach, plant and turn, the other the push-off and the transition into the stroke; if it is to be taught correctly, it is advisable to teach and coach with this in mind. The head is the main lever to be considered, for if the head moves on the wall its influence will create resistances in the push-off stage. It is the controlling

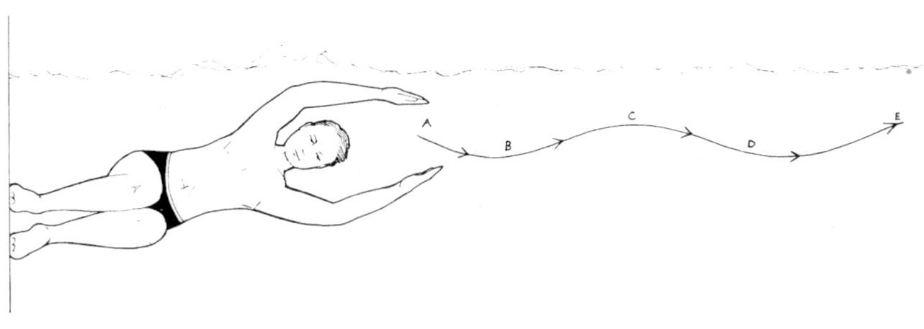

Fig 42 The undulating path away from the wall in the 'push-off' and 'transition into stroke'.

Fig 43a   A controversial stage of the breaststroke turn is the synchronization of head and arm movements during the arm cycle. Initially the swimmer leaves the wall in the first sequence of downward undulation.

Fig 43d   As the forceful insweep continues, the head comes up to its highest position; this causes the body to curve, with the feet and legs moving upwards.

Fig 43b   During the outward sweep of the arms the head starts to rise.

Fig 43e   The arms accelerate forcefully backwards, and the head contributes emphasis and power by dipping downwards. These two actions reverse the curve of the body. This 'principle of movement', will occur without any movement from the hips.

Fig 43c   The head continues to rise, a movement which enables the powerful upper body muscle groups to create greater power in the insweep of the arms.

niques, particularly breaststroke because it traces out an undulating path away from the wall.

Controversial Aspects of the Breaststroke Turn

factor for even greater distance away from the wall, and it also dictates how much reactive movement there is of the feet.

Both butterfly and breaststroke require substantial water depth for turning tech-

We have already observed (Chapter 5, breaststroke) that much greater power can be created by muscle groups of the upper body if the body is in a higher position. Similarly in the underwater sequence, greater power and therefore distance in the turn can be attained if the head and upper body is nominally raised. However, this leads to complications with man-made laws; analysing the turn clarifies the stage which can be controversial. With reference to Fig 42, as the swimmer leaves the wall it is important that a depth of at least a metre is achieved, for during the path from B to C the body will rise because the head and upper body is raised; the main reason for this is that in the higher position the powerful muscles of the upper body can be used to best advantage during the 'insweep' in this stage of the arm action and will therefore create greater power and distance in the turn. As a consequence of this movement, however, the body curves (see Fig 43d), the feet and head being higher than the mid-portion of the body.

From C to D the arms accelerate backwards and the head drops rapidly downwards, and these two actions create a 'piking' of the body in the opposite direction (downwards), so both head and feet move downwards. When viewed from above, an official may see the dolphin-like movement of the feet and consider it to be an action which merits disqualification; in many cases, however, it is mainly 'sympathetic' and is not deliberate. If no head and body movement occurs, then there cannot be any reactionary movement of the legs.

If the head and body movement is modified, then how much the feet react is relative to the amount of modification. This will have a proportional and detrimental effect on the distance which can be gained from the wall in the turn. Controversy reigns amongst officials concerning this one aspect of the turn, and at big events even underwater cameras shy away from showing the complete turn. If any changes are to be contemplated, then it can only come from a change in FINA law. Any change in this phase of the turn will enhance both the stroke and the times applicable to the event.

The Normal Breaststroke Turn

Fig 44a   In breaststroke and butterfly turns both hands touch the wall simultaneously.

Fig 44b   The hand on the turning side now leaves the wall as the legs flex into the midriff and the feet start to cross over.

Fig 44c   The lower hand now starts to pull upwards; it is one of the three factors which contribute to maintaining depth in progress away from the wall. The body is side on and starts to 'knife' into the water gaining depth; the feet are in the 'crucifix' position.

Fig 44d   The major contributor to depth – the touching hand – now 'javelins' over the centre line of the body and enters deeply bringing the body downwards.

Fig 44g   The breaststroke 'pull-out' takes place with an outward and inward sculling action.

Fig 44e   With the body completely on its side, the legs extend and push powerfully away from the wall.

Fig 44h   The hands are pushed back strongly in an accelerating action throughout, with the body perfectly streamlined.

Fig 44f   The body spirals onto the breast position, perfectly streamlined with one hand on top of the other and the head cushioned between the biceps.

Fig 44i   The hands recover close to the body turning palm upwards so bringing the elbows inward; this creates even less resistance to forward motion.

Approach

Both hands reach for the wall so as to touch simultaneously; on the turning side, one hand is lower than the other. The body comes up high in the water, and the swimmer inhales.

Plant

The fingers touch first, followed by the palm of the hand with the fingertips pointing upwards. According to the speed of the approach, the elbow bends and continues to flex until the head is close to the wall. Underwater the knees bend and the feet come together, the instep of one foot tucking into the sole of the other (this is the crucifix position, and minimizes resistance). The body is upright, and the eyes must be fixed rigidly on the touching hand. One arm leaves the wall with the palm of the hand turned towards the hip and brushing against it before it gains depth and starts to extend forwards (away from the wall).

Turn and Push-off

In a co-ordinated movement the upper body and the arm push vigorously away from the wall, the back of the head leading. The trailing hand turns palm upwards, and from a depth pulls upwards against the pressure of water; the touching hand leaves the wall, thumb downwards. Initially the eyes follow the touching hand as it traces a straight path over the head, then 'javelins' deep into the water. In a co-ordinated movement the feet are planted on the wall (for an instant neither hand nor feet are in contact with the wall); they then push forcefully away from the wall with the body still on its side and the arms together in a streamlined movement.

Transition into the Stroke

The body spirals onto the breast as the arms commence their stroke cycle. The head and upper body movements are synchronized throughout with the arm cycle. The body and head move nominally upwards during the outward and inward sweep of the arm action then once the hands are vigorously pushed through below the hips, a reverse downward movement takes place. As the speed of the glide declines, the legs start their cycle at the same time as the hands are recovered close to the body, palms uppermost. As the hands pass the swimmer's face, the head is raised, in synchronized timing with the arms as they extend ahead. They incline upwards and, followed by the upper body, break the surface of the water; oxygen is then taken during the insweep of the first arm cycle. From the moment the hands come into contact with the wall to the time the head breaks the surface of the water, approximately four seconds should have elapsed. The transition into the general stroke cycle should then be immediate and smooth.

Breaststroke Turn Practices

1. The swimmers line up holding the rail along the pool side. Practices should start with the 'throw-away' turn sequence.
2. The swimmers hold the rail and float in the water, and practise a shallow alternating kick.
3. Next the swimmer might bend the elbows and raise the body, bringing the head up close to the wall. The arm on the turning side releases the rail and drops down in the water with the palm of the hand towards the hip, brushing against the hip and gaining depth; it then starts to extend forwards (away from the wall) and pulls upwards towards the surface of

the water (pulling the body downwards).

4. The eyes must be kept on the touching hand holding the rail constantly.

5. The teaching point for 2, 3 and 4 should be 'pull-up'. Look out for any perceptible head movement; this must be prevented.

6. Repeat the above practices and also include bringing the feet onto the wall in the crucifix position; bend the legs at the knees and bring the knees up to the midriff.

7. The following exercise has the teaching point of 'fall-back': the touching hand leaves the wall rail, and the feet make contact on the wall; the back of the head hits the water, with the touching arm tracing a linear arc over the back part of the head. The blade of the hand enters the water, thumb first.

8. The way the hand enters the water is the single greatest contributor to depth. It must not be just thrown in, but must cut in as deeply as possible; the best instruction to use for this is to tell swimmers to 'javelin' into the water.

9. With the swimmers now facing away from the wall, instruct them to drop down, push off vigorously and synchronize the head and body movement to the underwater arm cycle.

10. In the underwater phase, as the hands recover forwards the swimmer synchronizes lifting the head, which brings the body to the surface.

11. The swimmers again face the wall, and swim in from two metres practising the whole turn.

12. The complete turn may be timed and a whistle blown as the head emerges.

MEDLEY TURNS

In the execution of any turn, the more skilful will always win that extra fraction of a second, and this is especially important when in these days of electronic timing, when events are won or lost by hundredths of a second. Any turn therefore demands greater consideration and inspired technique than ever before. In the individual events there have been innovations in turn techniques – for instance in breaststroke and back crawl – but the medley event appears to be the poor relation; coverage is sparse even in the principal magazines covering swimming techniques.

The butterfly to back crawl leg of a medley is probably of less concern, but the back-to-breast turn is undoubtedly significant because these strokes are the slowest legs of the individual medley. If techniques could be improved in these sections of the event then the gain in time could be of great importance.

BUTTERFLY TO BACK CRAWL TURN –

This turn is simple to understand and to implement. The swimmer comes from a position of frontal resistance, although the undulating character of butterfly reduces frontal profile resistance (during the swim) – relative, of course, to the efficiency of the swimmer involved. However, when pushing away from the wall, the broad area of the back presents significant resistance; by minimizing this, transition into the stroke is much quicker and more efficient. It is accomplished by one shoulder dipping away from the wall, at the same time as the opposite arm lifts the elbow particularly high. The blade of the hand 'javelins' into the water and sculls ahead, linking up with the other arm which is extended ahead. Thus the body 'knifes' away into the water, instead of presenting the highly resistant area of the back pushing away from the wall.

Coaching Practices for the Breaststroke Turn

Coaching Phases	*Coaching Practices/Points*
Approach	Swim in and touch simultaneously
Plant	1. Keep up incoming speed by adjusting movement of the elbow bend 2. Forehead stops short of the wall with eyes on touching hand 3. Arm on turning side moves downwards, hand touches hip before extending ahead
Turn and push off	1. Extended arm-pulls upwards; body 'knifes' away from the wall; touching arm arcs above head and 'javelins' into the water 2. Back of the head contacts water first (not the ear) 3. Feet in 'crucifix' position, then contact the wall 4. Arms join the extension ahead (hand on hand) 5. Body completely on its side as it leaves the wall 6. Body now spirals onto the breast position
Transition into stroke	1. Synchronize up and down head and body movements with arm action 2. As the hands recover forwards and upwards the head is also raised to bring the body to the surface

Fig 45a   In the butterfly to back crawl turn, the swimmer approaches the wall increasing or decreasing the length of stroke as necessary.

Fig 45b   The hands make contact with the wall, and the arms fold and bend according to the incoming speed. The right shoulder drops, with the right hand leading the body into extension.

Fig 45c Above the water surface the turn is similar to the breaststroke turn sequence, with the hand coming off the wall and passing straight over the central body line before entering the water.

Fig 45f The body is streamlined and gains maximum effect from the speed in the glide phase of the turn.

Fig 45d The left hand 'javelins' into the water and joins the right hand in extension ahead.

Fig 45g As the speed from the wall decreases to swimming speed, the swimmer dolphin kicks, raises the head and surfaces for the normal back crawl leg of the medley.

Fig 45e One hand goes on top of the other and the legs begin to straighten and push powerfully away from the wall.

The turn also equates with the rule covering back crawl in that the body is never guilty of being the full 90 degrees from the supine position.

BACK CRAWL TO BREASTSTROKE TURN

When I was the coach at Guildford City ASC one of my swimmers expressed some apprehension concerning the turn from back to breaststroke relating to the oxygen debt that occurred during the change of stroke. In Britain at that time the most popular turn from back to breast was the reverse somersault turn. However, it was known to create problems in orientation and in the high degree of oxygen debt, and above all else it was slow. A turn was devised which consisted of a proportion of the old back crawl turn, with a flip-over or spin into the on-breast position. The turn required a vigorous hip movement with the feet thrown over the water onto the wall; after this had taken place, the swimmer would spin back onto the breast position. The turn was called the 'spin-over' turn, and after some logical progressive practices swimmers had little difficulty in mastering it. Its main advantages were that it created less oxygen debt; greater effort and distance could be gained in the under-water breaststroke sequence; it led to better orientation in finding the wall; and finally, it was faster.

To perform it, the swimmer would approach the wall on back crawl; if using the right arm he would spin into the turn to his left. Referring to Fig 46d and Fig 46e, the swimmer executes a fast circular rotation (sideways), then half-twists to the right, spinning onto the breast position to commence the stroke cycle.

Coaching the Back-to-Breast Spin-over Turn

1. The swimmer comes into the wall on back crawl. The touching arm crosses the centre line of the body with the hand planted on the wall (the fingers should be parallel to and just under the surface of the water).
2. The head moves away from the touching arm. Note that it is the hand being planted on the wall across the centre line, together with the head movement away from the touching arm, which creates the initial sideways rotational movement.
3. Practices may be employed in open water with the feet being thrown above and around the surface of the water, for

instance the spinning movement.
4. The swimmer comes into the wall, and as the hand makes contact with the wall the upper body comes up high; the swimmer almost assumes a sitting position in the water, then throws the feet vigorously over the water and onto the wall.
5. Underwater the trailing hand gives balance and assistance to the swivel movement.
6. The swimmer 'spins' back into the turn, leaving the wall 'side on'; the trailing hand pulls upwards to aid the depth factor.
7. The touching arm now 'javelins' into the water; this promotes depth, speed away from the wall and a faster 'on-breast' body position.
8. The legs straighten vigorously; the body is streamlined, with one hand on top of the other.
9. Now perfectly on breast, the swimmer commences the under-water breaststroke cycle.
10. It is important that the hands are recovered palm upwards and close to the body. As the leg drive backwards takes place, the head and arms incline upwards; this brings the body to the surface and ensures a smooth transition into the breaststroke leg of the medley.

In the individual medley event a fast transition from one stroke to another is of paramount importance, more so in the back-to-breast changeover sequence than in any other. The swimmer who achieves a lower oxygen debt in this section of the event will have greater transition speeds and will gain more distance in the breaststroke underwater sequence.

Fig 46a   The swimmer approaches the wall, reaching for it with her right hand just under the surface of the water.

Fig 46e   The arm now 'javelins' forcefully into the water, promoting depth, speed away from the wall and a faster 'on-breast' position.

Fig 46b   The legs flex into the abdomen thus keeping the pivoting arc small. This action is assisted by a fast hip movement.

Fig 46f   A vigorous push-off takes place with the arms extended ahead and the head lowered, ensuring still greater depth in the initial path away from the wall.

Fig 46c   The feet are almost in contact on the wall with the swimmer still taking in oxygen. The left hand now sculls upwards giving balance and assistance throughout the spinning phase of the turn.

Fig 46g   The swimmer is now perfectly 'on breast' and commences her breaststroke underwater cycle.

Fig 46d   The swimmer now twists out of the turning movement and over onto her side. The left hand continues the sculling action, pressing against the water and fully assisting each movement in its turn.

Fig 46h   Recovery of the hands must be close to the body as she kicks and surfaces for the breaststroke leg of the medley.

8

Stroke, Start and Turn Analysis

Stroke, start and turn analysis is one of the more interesting aspects of any teaching and coaching course. It is important to have an extensive knowledge in those areas, and analysis gives the lay coach or teacher greater insight into and understanding of each separate section. Stroke analysis provides both the tutored and the untutored with a greater concept of the stroke both above the water and – more important still – under its surface.

STROKE ANALYSIS

The analytical approach is to group the components into a format which we should recognize from any teaching and coaching syllabus, namely: body – leg action – arm action – breathing – timing. Under examination conditions, the swimmer being analysed swims six lengths with one minute between each length; each of the lengths should relate to one section of the format, with one extra length. At the end of the six lengths there will be a further few minutes to complete the analysis. The main drawback to this system is that whilst engaged on one section, you may recognize a major fault in another and lose concentration. However, you must fix your mind on the original section and evaluate what you see at that particular moment in time.

The analysis itself must observe certain criteria:

• Organize the format so that in each length the analysis concentrates on just one part of the stroke.
• Use the final length for a section you consider important and which requires further detail, for example arm action.
• Draw 'stick men' if you can, then transcribe the information you need from this graphical synopsis as and when you have the time.
• Note that comments such as 'good body position' or 'good efficient leg/arm action' are opinions: you are required to put down exactly what you see, and not what you think is good in the stroke.

When referring to each of the components the following should be observed:

• First, the relationship between the water level and the head.
• Analyse from limb extremities.
• Observe the arm entry in relation to the shoulder or centre line.

• Observe how the breathing cycle relates to the arm cycle. Note that the breathing cycle takes place throughout the complete arm cycle; it is inhalation that occurs late in the inward scull, as in breaststroke.

• Timing relates to the number of leg movements to one complete arm cycle; or as in breaststroke, the number of separate component actions in the whole stroke cycle: pull – breathe – kick and glide.

The following examples of stroke analysis would be based on a swimmer with ideal technique, and in a competitive type of stroke may be analysed and written in the way set out below.

FRONT-CRAWL ANALYSIS ————

Body Position

The water level is to the forehead, with the body inclined to give a good efficient kick. There are longitudinal movements as each hand sinks to 'catch' and the head is turned for inhalation.

Leg Action

The kick comes from the hip, acts down through the knee, which bends due to the pressure of water and to the timing of the levers in the kick down. It finishes at the feet, which are plantar-flexed and - whip-like in their action. The leg action is alternating with the legs working close together; note that the number of kicks per cycle relates to the timing and is not to be associated with the leg action.

Arm Action

From the 'catch' position the hands flex slightly and then scull outwards, backwards, downwards and inwards. They now trace a path which is slightly outwards and back to the end of the costume, with the little finger exiting the water first. The whole sculling pattern is in the form of a shallow 'S'. The recovery of the arm has the elbow in a high position. The entry of the hand in the water is approximately 45cm in front of and in line with the shoulder. The hand then extends ahead and sinks to catch.

Breathing

The breathing cycle is bilateral, with trickle exhalation and inhalation in a trough near the end of the push phase.

Timing

There are six kicks to one complete arm cycle with continuity of arm and leg movements.

BACK-CRAWL ANALYSIS ————

Body Position

The water level is at the ear, and the body is inclined enough to give a good efficient kick. There are both longitudinal and lateral movements as the hands sink to 'catch' and the arms trace a sideways sculling path.

Leg Action

The kick comes from the hip region and acts down through the knee, which bends due to the pressure of water and to the timing of the levers in the kick up. It finishes at the feet which are plantar-flexed and whip-like in their action. The leg action is alternating, with the legs working close together.

Arm Action

From a deep 'catch' position the hands flex slightly, then scull outwards, upwards and backwards. When level with the head the elbow starts to bend and continues to do so until it attains an angle of approximately 90 degrees throughout the 'push' phase of the inward scull. It finishes in a downward movement below the hip. The arm now travels upwards, to exit from the water with the thumb or back of the hand leading. As the arm recovers in a straight arc, the hand turns to present the little finger on entry, in line and ahead of the shoulder, and sinks to a deep 'catch'.

Breathing

The breathing cycle is explosive, with inhalation on the recovery of one arm and exhalation on the recovery of the other.

Timing

There are six kicks to one complete arm cycle, with continuous arm and leg movements.

BREASTSTROKE ANALYSIS ————

Body Position

When the arms and legs are fully extended the body is almost horizontal and using an undulating action, the head and legs rising and falling throughout the whole phase of the cycle. Both leg and arm movements are simultaneous, with arm and body movements continuous throughout the stroke.

Leg Action

From an extended position, the feet are recovered to and within hip width until the upper limb is approximately 140 degrees to the main trunk. The feet now dorsiflex and the kick is outwards, backwards, downwards then inwards until they come together in a plantar-flexed position.

Arm Action

From an extended position, the hands flex slightly and the scull is outwards, downwards and backwards with the arms in a position of 'high elbow'; the inward scull continues until the fingertips almost meet. Throughout the complete arm cycle there is a continuous angular movement of the hands: as the arms extend forwards, the hands turn to face downwards and then outwards as they reach full extension and 'catch'.

Breathing

The breathing cycle is explosive, with inhalation taking place during the inward scull, and exhalation occurring throughout the rest of the stroke cycle.

Timing

Pull – breathe – kick, with little or no glide.

BUTTERFLY ANALYSIS ————

Body Position

The body performs an undulating movement throughout the complete stroke cycle; the head hyper-extends during inhalation, then moves down until the chin touches the chest. Both leg and arm movements are simultaneous and continuous.

Leg Action

From a depth of approximately 60cm the legs move up to the surface together. The upper legs now drop, with the lower legs continuing to the surface, thus giving an angular vee-like shape between the upper and lower limbs. The downward movement is generated at the hips with the lower legs thrusting downwards together until they are back in line with the upper leg. This action gives propulsive power and also raises the hips.

Arm Action

From an extended position, the hands flex slightly and scull outwards, then upwards, downwards, backwards and inwards in a continuous angular movement. The arms are in a position of 'high elbow' before the hands make inward contact, they turn backwards and push through to the hips with the little finger exiting for a ballistic-type recovery of the arms close to the surface of the water. The thumbs enter the water first, ahead of and in line with the shoulder. They then sink to 'catch' ready for the next stroke cycle.

Breathing

The breathing cycle is explosive, the swimmer inhaling near the end of every second 'push' phase with the head hyperextended close to the surface of the water; exhalation occurs throughout the remainder of each arm cycle.

Timing

This is a two-beat leg action, the main kick occurring as the hands fall to 'catch', and the second at the end of the push phase.

GENERAL OBSERVATION ——————

A competent stroke analysis will make you aware of faults as well as good stroke technique; all swimmers have strengths and weaknesses in each stroke and it is important to transcribe exactly what you see. Then evaluate the analysis and teach or coach on the prevailing weaknesses. A serious fault will not be put right over a short period of time, and exercises to correct it will have to be included in the 'sectional' part of the schedule and perhaps in the warm-up too.

Stroke analysis is both interesting and stimulating. It helps to improve knowledge of the stroke, and fosters an intuitive flair for the correction of prevalent faults. The corrective formula could be a better known coaching point or points, or it could lead to a completely new concept in your coaching repertoire. Whichever way you choose to rectify the problem, it will give you satisfaction and more confidence in your own ability as a coach.

EXAMPLES OF ASSESSMENT FORMS

The following are examples of stroke, start and turn assessment sheets, showing exactly what the coach should be looking for.

Stroke Analysis

Date.........................   *Stroke*...................

Swimmer...................   *D.O.B*.................

Body Position Look for: head position; body movements; breathing.

Leg Action Is the movement from the hips? Is the knee bend correct? Are the feet plantar-/dorsiflexed? Is it circular?

Arm Action Look for: entry/extension/ flexion; sculling/straight line; recovery/ 'catch-up'.

Breathing Where does breathing occur in the arm action? Is it smooth/late/uni/ bilateral?

Timing Look for the number of kicks to each arm cycle. Fly/breast cyclical.

Coach:.....................

Start Analysis

Stance Use stick men throughout. Show the angle of the legs, was it 140 degrees between the upper and the lower leg? Are the toes gripping the edge of the block? Do the hands grab the block inside or outside the feet? Indicate the head position. In back crawl are the feet together, or is one higher than the other? Are the arms straight or bent; the head back or tipped forwards?

Take-off Which moved first, head, arms or legs? Did the arms swing back and then forwards, or just forwards? Did they swing in a circle, and if they did, when did they stop and was it sudden? Was there a good drive off the block, was it explosive? In back crawl, which moved first, the head, arms, or legs? Did the hips lift or were they flat?

Flight (drive in back crawl) Was the flight upwards or downwards? Was the head too high or too low? Did the arms move in the flight? Was the back arched? Did the knees bend in flight (hitch-kick) then start to extend? In back crawl, indicate

the head action and the angle of the head; also the arm action, was it central up the body-line, or fan-like or flung to the side?

Entry Were the hands apart, or together on entry? Was the head up, down or at an angle? Was the body flat, or angled, was the entry clean? Were the legs straight or bent? What was the depth of entry? Backcrawl: as above

Transition into Stroke

Is the glide short or long? Was momentum lost? Was the first action leg, arm, or both together? When did the swimmer breathe? Was the transition smooth or weak? Back crawl: as above.

Summation *(type of start)* Grab/pike/ wind-up/hitch-kick/backcrawl. Analysis assessment forms can be formulated with some of the above points included in them. The candidate would be allowed six starts in order to assess completely the start in question.

Turn Analysis

Approach Indicate whether the approach was smooth and positive; whether the stroke shortened or lengthened. What was the breathing cycle? Show the leg action, was it dolphin, and strong or weak or none? Was it half-somersault and half-twist (front crawl), or half-twist and half-somersault (backstroke), and was it early or late?

Plant Check the arms and legs; was the shoulder dipped or straight? Did the body position rise or fall, and was it extended?

Turn Indicate whether the turn was left or right. Was the head steady or did it turn? Did the arms extend sufficiently and the hands pull up and javelin over the head; was there enough extension? Show the shoulder position, was the swimmer on his side or on breast?

Push-off Was the body on its side, or on breast? Did the head face on its side or look downwards? Were the arms, in extension, apart or together? Was the action explosive or weak?

Transition into stroke Was the glide long or short? Was the first action with the legs or the arms or together? Note the breathing cycle, when was breath taken; note whether the transition was smooth and efficient.

Summation *(type of turn)* Tumble turn/back-crawl flip-turn/reverse somersault turn/back-to-breast. Identify whether the turn was aggressive or weak.

9

Physiology and the Principles of Training

The body can be considered as a set of levers that are programmed by the neuro-muscular system of the body. Impulses from the brain travel down the spinal motor nerve, then to the muscle fibres that are served by that motor nerve. The levers of the body meet in joints that are held together by ligaments and tendons, which then join a greater mass of muscle. A signal from the brain will cause the muscle to contract, another will cause it to relax and extend. There are many thousands of fibres in a muscle, and they can be divided into two different types: fast twitch and slow twitch. If a single muscle contracts there will be linear movement of that lever, if a set of muscles contracts there will be either an outward movement referred to as 'abduction' or an inward movement, 'adduction'. The nerve impulses which stimulate the muscle fibres also cause energy to be released, resulting in a corresponding movement of the body's levers and thus progress through the water.

Two protein filaments, myosin and actin, also interact and cause the muscle fibres to contract, thus achieving movement of the levers. Only one chemical stored in the muscle is able to provide the energy for this interaction: ATP – adenosine triphosphate. P-Cr (creatine phos-phate) and glycogen are used to replace the energy lost by the ATP as it breaks down its own energy to supply the muscle fibres. A further source of energy and phosphate can be found in the break-down of fats; this is released through lipid metabolism and is a slower process for the contribution of energy.

In competitive swimming and especially sprint events, the demands for oxygen in muscular contraction cannot be fully met. Muscle contractions therefore require phosphagen levels which are supplied to the fast-twitch fibres through the two anaerobic systems. Three complementary energy systems are commonly involved in this resynthesis process: the first two are referred to as anaerobic (independent of, or without oxygen and instantaneous in their action), the third is aerobic and slower in its reproductive action (with oxygen).

The first system (ATP – P-Cr) can only supply the energy in muscular contraction for a limited period of time (five to ten seconds) and the cost in supplying that energy causes the ATP to lose one phosphate; this phosphate is reinstated through the energy systems of the body. The second energy system (lactate energy system) now cuts in and supplies the energy requirements for a further period of time; and when this is exhausted the athlete must rely on the third energy system. In this system oxygen is constantly present supplying an abundance of energy to the slow-twitch fibres but at a slower rate. The three energy systems are therefore:

1. The ATP – P-Cr (creatine phosphate) system
2. The anaerobic lactic acid (glycolysis) system
3. The aerobic (oxygen utilization) system

In the ATP – P-Cr system, the breakdown of CATP (creatine ATP) to CADP (creatine di-phosphate) leads to the release of energy. P-Cr is now required for the synthesis of ATP from ADP in order to provide further energy.

In the second energy system, ATP is now replaced by energy from the anaerobic phase of glycolysis ('glycol' = glucose, and 'lysis' means 'the splitting of'), where glycogen is broken down to glucose and subsequently further to pyruvic acid. This process provides a rapid supply of energy for the resynthesis of ADP to ATP and the swimmer can continue to sprint at almost top speed for a further forty to fifty seconds. Unfortunately the principal by-product of this process is lactic acid which steadily builds up in the body leading to a lowering of pH in the blood. This increases the acidity of the body fluids and creates progressive exhaustion, as waste products cause exhaustion to set in. When physical activity continues at an excessively high rate, the level of lactic acid will rise to a level which prevents further muscular work taking place resulting in cramp and at worst collapse.

Oxygen metabolizes lactic acid and resaturates the myoglobin (a substance similar to haemoglobin). If we exercise strenuously, our bodies incur what is known as an 'oxygen debt'. This must be repaid after the high level of physical activity by a period of rest and rapid deep breathing (flat-out aerobic exertion can increase the oxygen uptake from, say, 250ml at rest to over five litres, an increase of twenty times). There are three systems which effect the removal of lactic acid:

1. Lactic acid in skeletal muscle is released in the blood, and transported to the liver where some of it is converted back to glucose by a process known as the Cori cycle.
2. Some is neutralized by 'buffer' systems in the muscle fibres. In the blood it combines with bicarbonate and dissociates into CO_2 (which is removed in the lungs) and water.
3. The remaining lactic acid may be removed by being taken up by adjacent muscle fibres, or by other groups of less active muscles. There, the lactic acid converts to pyruvic acid, which then enters the Krebs cycle (see later section, 'The Aerobic Oxygen-Utilization System) whose end products are CO_2 and water.

In the third energy system (aerobic), glycogen is again converted to glucose, which is further broken down to carbon dioxide and water by utilizing oxygen. Oxygen comprises 21 per cent of the air we breathe; it passes out of the blood and into the muscle fibres saturating the myoglobin, and is conveyed to the mitochondria (distribution centres for ATP) where it is used to release energy for muscle contraction.

In the aerobic system of exercise, oxygen metabolizes the lactic acid for the regeneration of chemical energy into mechanical energy, in other words muscle contraction. It is a slower and more economical system of energy production, providing about 40 per cent of the energy for the 100m swim, and between 50 per cent and 60 per cent of the energy in middle distance swimming. Exercise can be continued almost indefinitely, as the oxygen supply to the muscle is sufficient for the metabolic processes (to the slow-twitch fibres) to take place.

When visualizing these energy systems one thinks of them as separate entities, because they cut in one after the other. There are stages, however, when all three energy systems are working in conjunction with one another, the aerobic cycle working flat out to contribute its share (Fig 47 indicates how each system may work in conjunction with the others). Each system is just as important as the others and a training programme must include work on each one.

It is virtually a physical impossibility to swim any race over 25m without taking in oxygen. Every time this function occurs, the aerobic system (the third energy system) makes its contribution, but with the predominant source being either ATP – P-Cr, or anaerobic glycolosis. On most occasions, oxygen is present in many places throughout the body, for example in the lungs – haemoglobin is the oxygen-carrying pigment in the red blood cells, and there are 280ml in arterial blood and 800ml in venous blood. Oxygen passes through the capillary wall, across the interstitial fluid to the muscle cell membrane, then into the muscle cell where it reaches the myoglobin and progresses through the mitochondrial membrane. Even though there is a continual presence of oxygen at a high level of sprinting, the aerobic system on its own is not fast enough in supplying the muscular energy requirements in comparison to both anaerobic systems.

Many coaches and teachers find the three energy systems difficult to interpret in terms of a swimming event. A theoretical analogy based on a 100m front crawl event may make the energy systems

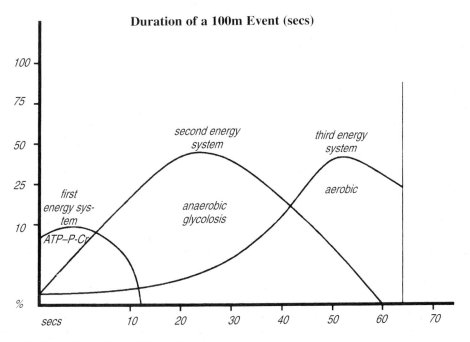

Fig 47 *Indicating the contribution of each energy system.*

easier to understand. Thus a hypothetical race situation may be as follows:

• The stroke in question is front crawl, the distance 100m, and the swim time 63.0 seconds.
• Surmise that at the start the swimmer gains 6m without a stroke cycle and 12m at the turn (gaining 1m with the flip-over and 3m off the wall), in total 18m.
• If 18m is subtracted from 100m it would give a DPS (distance per stroke) of 1.3m (82 divided by 63.0 secs being the swim time).
• Assume that the swimmer covers 1.3m with each stroke cycle. A breathing cycle will cover one stroke cycle. The number of times the swimmer will breathe during each of the four lengths will give a contributory and an aerobic factor (the third energy system).

Example: The swimmer breathes (strokes) 11 on the first 25m, 42 on the next 50m and 18 on the last 25m; this gives 71 breathing cycles at 1.3m per cycle.

On a flat-out 100m event 8 per cent would be fuelled by the ATP – P-Cr, 52 per cent by the anaerobic glycolosis, and 40 per cent in an aerobic form.

It would be far simpler to equate each of the systems as separate entities, for this would give percentages and greater comprehension; when they work in conjunction it creates the problem of where one concludes and another takes over, and assumptions have to be made in order to achieve a clearer understanding. The ATP – P-Cr system would be expended on the first length, with the anaerobic glycolosis and the aerobic systems continuing to fuel muscular movement until the event was completed. These two systems operate together for the final three lengths of

the event but in varying proportions. The example below ('The Three Energy Systems in Race Conditions') may give a clearer picture of energy metabolism in a race situation.

It also shows that all three energy systems are of equal importance and the coach must place equal emphasis on the training of each individual system. The untrained swimmer will have low levels of technique and therefore lower percentage levels in distance per stroke; the levels in all three systems will also be lower, and the event would have to be swum at a slower rate. An improvement in these levels can be made with the appropriate sets, distances and target times. In the highly trained swimmer the glycogen levels in the muscle are sufficient to last most races without having to draw on the 'back-up' glycogen store in the liver and in the fats in the body. These 'back-up' levels are used up in the longer training situations, which create even greater levels of efficiency.

If there is one system that may be neglected more than the others, that system must be the ATP – P-Cr system (first energy system). The training effect of this is short-lived, however, so this type of training is usually catered for in the 'competitive' period. It should be made up of sets over short distances, 15 to 20m only. Every set should comprise flat-out swims, and rest intervals which may be active, passive or 'walk-backs'. An active rest swim can be a push-off from the wall, a pulse check after the swim followed by a swim down, then a tumble-turn into the next swim. Passive swims will result in a lower heart rate. The recovery rate of phosphagen is from thirty seconds to full recovery in five minutes, and it goes without saying that the trained swimmer will recover in less time than the untrained.

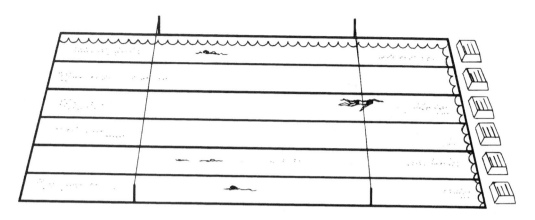

Fig 48   The first energy system (5 to 10 seconds; 8 per cent of the race).

THE THREE ENERGY SYSTEMS IN RACE CONDITIONS

The ATP – C-Pr System

The ATP – C-Pr (creatine phosphate) system is the first energy system in a 100m event. Anaerobic means 'without oxygen', and at anaerobic levels of swimming the body is working at levels when its oxygen requirements cannot be met by its oxygen transport system. In this situation two proteins, actin and myosin, are drawn into one another by a movement which results in a contraction of muscle: ATP provides the energy for this movement, after which ATP breaks down to ADP.

ATP — ADP + P + energy for contraction
ADP + P-Cr ————— ATP
                  (utilizing the CP
                  in the muscle)

Metabolism takes place within the muscle in the first energy system. Hypothetically this system is expended as the swimmer reaches the above position in the swim. If the number of breathing cycles is calculated, they will indicate the contributory aerobic factor in the first phase of the swim, ie eleven. The ATP – P-Cr system

comprises 8 per cent of the race and is expended at the second set of turning flags. At this moment in time anaerobic glycolosis – the second energy system – takes over.

The Anaerobic Lactate Energy System

This system replaces energy (ATP) in the muscle from the anaerobic phase of glycolosis. Glycogen from the liver is broken down to glucose and then to pyruvic acid; it is a process for providing a rapid supply of energy for the resynthesis of ADP to ATP in the muscle. Unfortunately without the presence of oxygen the principal by-product of this is lactic acid

ATP + Contraction ——————————ADP
Glycogen —Glucose —Pyruvic acid + ADP— ATP
          Pyruvic acid – O_2 ——————Lactic acid

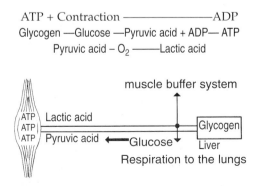

Fig 49   The anaerobic lactate energy system.

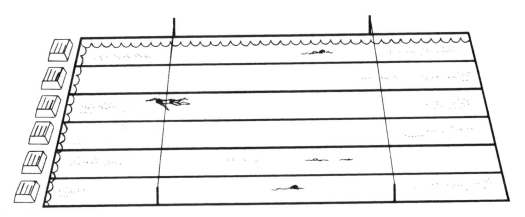

Fig 50   The second energy system (52 per cent of the race).

which lowers the pH; these levels will increase until exhaustion sets in.

The anaerobic glycolosis system contributes 52 per cent of the energy requirements, receiving a contribution throughout from the aerobic system as the swimmer breathes sixty times on the remaining three lengths.

The Aerobic Oxygen-Utilization System

Glycogen is again converted to glucose, and this is further broken down to pyruvic acid which is then converted to 'acetyl co-enzyme A' into the Krebs cycle. Fats also follow the same pathway. The Krebs, or citric acid, cycle is a complex cycle of enzyme-controlled reactions in which pyruvic acid (in the presence of oxygen) is broken down into carbon dioxide, and ATP is synthesized. The cycle provides the final step in the oxidation of carbohydrates and glycogen, these having been broken down during glycolosis to – amongst other things – pyruvic acid. It also deals with the final phases of fat oxidation, and is concerned in the synthesis of some amino acids.

The cycle is associated with the mitrochondria, which contain the system of enzymes. The Krebs cycle releases energy slowly but in abundance, and a well trained athlete's body will be able to conserve glycogen by using a greater percentage of fat. Aerobic work should provide about 40 per cent of the energy required for the 100m swim, and the proportion of aerobic energy for an event lasting from two to three minutes would be about 55 per cent.

The Anaerobic Threshold

A good endurance programme ensures that in time a competitor will increase his total blood volume. At rest, venous blood contains approximately 12 per cent volume of oxygen (exercise will reduce this to lower levels). Aerobically the working muscle requires an adequate supply of oxygen. Certain tests can assess the maximum uptake of oxygen (VO_2 max) and these are used to assess a competitor's aerobic performance. In view of this, the aerobic training programme should be drawn up in full knowledge and consideration of the competitor's ability to sustain a pre-determined workload or set.

If a training level could be built into the programme by which lactic acid and

'VO$_2$ max' could be maintained at optimum aerobic levels, a highly efficient aerobic programme would result. This can be achieved by ensuring a set of work in the region of 4mmol/l blood lactate. It is a level we refer to as the 'anaerobic threshold' and is a stage where the work rate goes through the aerobic ceiling into the anaerobic state. It achieves a continuous programme and set of work so that training levels are maintained at the desired norm. If the level of sustained work is wrongly calibrated and is higher than this threshold, then the athlete will not be able to cope.

A very important point is that when glucose is used by the muscle (or any) cell, it is always metabolized down to pyruvic acid. If there is enough oxygen, then the pyruvic acid automatically goes into the Krebs cycle. If there is not enough oxygen, or if the demands are too high to be met by the aerobic system even when it is working at maximum capacity, then the pyruvic acid is converted to lactic acid. This factor allows more glucose to be metabolized (anaerobically), so achieving a better level of energy from the glucose molecule. Anaerobically, only two molecules of ATP are attained out of one molecule of glucose (compared to thirty-six aerobically); so the aerobic system is eighteen times more efficient. There are, however, far more anaerobic enzymes in the muscle cell (especially in the fast-twitch fibres), so in absolute terms, four times the energy levels can be generated anaerobically as compared to aerobically.

Front crawl was chosen in the preceding example more for simplicity than for any other reason. The distance per stroke was a main consideration, but the DPS for both butterfly and breaststroke is far greater. It should also be remembered that even at minimal speeds, the oxygen

Lactic Acid Levels

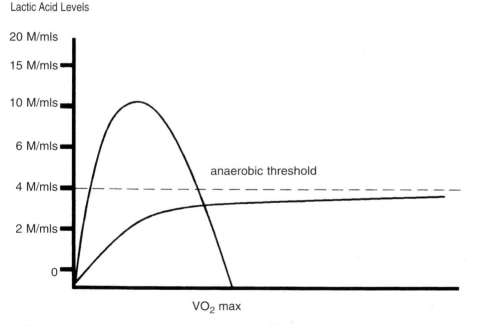

Fig 51

Guide Table for Practical Sessions				
Heart Rate Zone	*Max H.R.*	*Duration/Mins*	*System*	*Pace*
60%	130/140	60+	Lipid Metab	Minimal
80%	170/180	15/30	An threshold	Hard
90%	190/200	10/15	An glycolosis	Sub max
100%	210/220	5/8	CP/ATP	Max

uptake and heart rates increase accordingly for back crawl, butterfly and breaststroke, in that order; breaststroke in particular has an oxygen uptake of almost twice that of front crawl, with the heart rate increasing by almost another forty to fifty beats per minute (Costill). The example was used on a coaching course and successfully explained a vital area of science that many have viewed with a certain amount of trepidation.

This newly acquired understanding was reinforced with a six-day programme, comprising a four-day level of anaerobic threshold and then two days progression on the other two systems. Progressive training was accomplished through logical scheduling based on pulse rates only. The table above was used as a guide for the practical pool sessions, with the maximum heart rate stated to be 220 BPM.

SPECIFICITY OF TRAINING ─────

In order to derive the greatest possible effect from a programme of training, it must include work and progression in each of the energy systems. Every athlete has a percentage of both fast-twitch and slow-twitch fibre content in the muscle. The proportions of each never change, but research has indicated that it is possible to train fast-twitch fibres to take on the characteristics of slow-twitch fibres; this could mean these fibres take in oxygen and work for longer periods with a greater facility for metabolizing lactic acid, and for removing it. It could also be one reason why in a competitive event the aerobic system works in conjunction with or parallel with the anaerobic systems.

It is now over fifteen years since the Russian national coach described Russia's bio-chemical testing programme; he revealed that blood samples were taken from his swimmers every three weeks, and that the results were used to indicate the speeds at which those swimmers should be training. It suggested that for a swimmer to get the best possible effects from the aerobic energy system, he should train at a level where the work rate went from the aerobic ceiling through into the anaerobic state. Perhaps the greatest emphasis in latter years has been on this anaerobic threshold training level. It is sometimes referred to as the 'onset of blood lactate accumulation' (OBLA) – maybe a better name for it as it indicates that the training is for the aerobic energy system alone.

There has been much controversy as to where exactly this threshold level is, although agreement has been reached concerning the levels of lactic acid which are now considered to be between 1.5 and 4mml/l. As the swimmer becomes fitter then this level may increase, hence the requirement for periodic testing. It is the most scientific way of establishing the threshold, but it is costly and it requires a person who can interpret the results correctly. Descending swims achieve most of the objectives in an anaerobic threshold training set. The aims will not be met at all phases of the set, but in general the objectives can be reached with 'target times' and frequent pulse checks. Either each of the sets can descend until the pulse rate is reached: 3 x 4/5 x 100 RI 15/20 T.T. 170/180 pulse; or once the AT pulse rate is reached, hold the following swim sets at this pulse rate by target-timing each swim: 3 x 4/5 x 100 RI 15/20 hold TT? on 2nd and 3rd set.

Anaerobic Glycolosis

Otherwise known as the lactate/glycolosis energy system, anaerobic glycolosis can be achieved by fast interval training, progressive sets, negative splits, high quality repetitions, broken repetitions and link swims. Pulse rates should be in the region of 190/200 sub-maximal, with longer intervals of rest (3 mins/talk-back depending on the swimmer's fitness).

Creatine Phosphate Energy System

This is maximum power swimming, and only cursory attention is given it either because the AT system has achieved all the notoriety or because it was thought that lactate tolerance covered its significance. But if it is neglected in training the swimmer will have to go to the second energy system early in the race, and then try and hang on with aerobic finishing energy. The training effects of maximum power swimming are short in terms of time, and should therefore be introduced during the 'competitive' period of train-

ing (see next section). The swim distance is 15 to 20m (push-offs from the wall), and pulse rates are at a maximum, checked at the 'set' distance with a passive rest/walk back, or an active rest/swim-down, then a tumble turn into the next swim.

Many new scientific innovations have come to the fore over the past decade, and some coaches view these with distrust. One certainty emerges, however, and that is that there is no one sure method which alone produces the successful swimmer; the techniques of stroke, start and turn cannot be manufactured from the laboratory. Thus the type of schedule and its ingredients depend upon the experience of the particular coach and not the scientist; moreover a young age group swimmer has much to learn before the physiological concepts of the energy systems should be injected into his programme. In many cases this aspect is brought in far too soon, resulting in the 'burn out syndrome' and inferior techniques that may persist throughout a potentially illustrious career.

There are, nevertheless, many scientific applications that can, and should be used by the inventive coach, for they are useful additions to progress, for example the percentage of best times, blood lactate measurements, T 30s and heart rate monitoring; although admittedly there are disadvantages with any one of these applications. Many coaches will opt for the heart-rate monitoring method because it is simple and cheap, but it has its own disadvantages regarding preciseness. There are electronic pulse monitors available today that attach to the swimmer and read out to a wrist attachment, and can be put into computer storage; these are good, but for a number of swimmers they would be expensive. Knowing your swimmer/s is the greatest advantage of all, and over a period of time the correct schedules, sets and cyclical training routines will certainly help in this and are adequate reason for the practical coach to choose the heart-rate monitoring method.

Cyclical Training

This describes a recurring programme of training adapted by the coach to suit the requirements of a squad of swimmers. It should be constructed around the three energy systems over a period of such time as will achieve his specific objectives. Normally these are two 'peaks' every year, and the programme would include preparation, pre-competitive and competitive phases. A shorter cyclical routine may extend over a two-, three- or four-week period but would include a condensed version of the normal annual programme. On completion of the condensed version, the cycle is then repeated.

In order to distinguish the length of the training cycle, a long routine may be referred to as a 'macro-cycle' and a shorter one as 'micro'. In these days of recurring meets and galas, the micro-cycle works well and fulfils the demands of a heavy competitive programme as well as complementing each of the energy systems. A progressive programme of overload will ensure the following:

1. An all-round improvement of fitness.
2. The inflicted stress factor on the body induces change and the conditioning of the mind to accept and meet these new stress levels.

The attainment of fitness is of paramount importance. With training, the number of capillaries per square millimetre of muscle doubles, myoglobin could increase threefold and the mitrochondria could also increase in volume threefold. We must next consider how we train the swimmer after an adequate level of fitness is achieved: if we only ever train over distance with short-rest interval work, for example, there will be a negative effect in the shorter events. It depends on three things:

1. The event entered for and the training considerations.
2. The type of muscle fibre composition of the swimmer (slow twitch for endurance and fast twitch for sprints).
3. The relative stroke and swimming distance, ie the 50/100m and the 100/1,500m.

The coach must always be aware that sprints for 50 and 100m are anaerobic, and that anything from 100m onwards is mainly aerobic, and this is true of all strokes. Use more than one method of training, but overload on the swimmer's individual speciality. Thus the programme of work should seek to develop:

1. Stroke technique with an in-depth knowledge and the ability to perform with a high degree of efficiency in starts and turns with take-overs.
2. Fitness and endurance.
3. A strength factor with sprint ability.

A coach must develop knowledge in all these areas. He or she must understand specificity of training and the physiological changes that take place with training loads. One point to remember is that the body will go through certain changes in order to keep up a level of energy; in this respect endurance training which is attained over a long period will give greater stamina and better results than that attained over a short period of time. A coach should use both endurance and speed intelligently, and should therefore avoid training on one only.

Competitive Targets

A swimmer of high competitive quality can only be peaked twice a year. The year's competitive training programme should be based on selected championship dates, namely the 'short course' and the 'long course' national championships. Each of these training peaks is further divided into a three-part season, each stage identified as preparation, pre-competitive and competitive (this includes the taper period). Thus in the seasonal build-up the itinerary might look like this:

Short Course

September/October
(preparation)
Inter Club Galas
Speedo League
Final

October/December
(pre-competitive)
Designated
English schools

December/March
(Competitive)
Open Meets/
Counties
Short course
Champs
World Short
Course

Long Course

March/April
(preparation)
Open Designated
Meet

April/May
(pre-competitive)
Easter Swim Meets
ASA Courses

June/July
(competitive)
National/Age
Group
Championships

Preparation Phase

First Part: Emphasis is on the technique of the stroke/s: starts, turns and long swims with short rest interval work.
Second Part: Distance swims at slow/medium pace with short rest intervals.

Pre-Competitive Phase

Much harder work and more demanding with regard to pace: time holding swims, slight decrease in metres, 5 per cent more sectional work but still an emphasis on technique.

Competitive Phase

Work now hard and very demanding; much more pace/speed is introduced with longer intervals of rest. Less distance is covered: percentage swims, p.b. + 8/10 seconds, more broken swims and so on.

Work to a Plan

Decide on two important swims in the year and group the work around them. Allow only two days' rest for other, less important swims.

Annual Plan and Fitness Programme

Fig 52.

Plateau Training

Many club swimmers will not reach the higher levels of competition and will have a 'non-specific' programme of training. Rather, they will have small peaks when they swim at gala or graded meet level.

Subjection of the Body to a Training Load

Techniques should be mastered early on in the year, although if a level is not sustained then they will diminish as the swimmer is subjected to increased levels of overload. The body's general fitness and cardio-vascular system is improved by overload in distance work; but this must be done gradually otherwise the swimmer will reach a stage where he cannot keep pace with the regime. Once basic fitness is established, then the coach must organize the swimmer's programme according to his individual strengths and talents for either distance or sprint events. Remember, a programme that relates to speed only will build strength in the muscle for the improvement of short sprinting ability, and this will do little to help the aerobic factor and the capacity of the distance swimmer. Distance training will enable a swimmer to swim longer distances, but it will not result in the changes necessary to enable him or her to swim short distances at top speed.

Sprint training imposes a stress factor of short duration but it is much more intense than the longer and slower distance events. As a swimmer doubles his swimming speed, he quadruples the resistance factor (because it obeys the inverse square law). Sprints will cause the muscles to contract faster against the greater force. Endurance is the ability of the muscle groups, together with the heart, to become stronger and more effi-

cient in order to meet the demands of any event. If a high level of work is imposed on the body the outer membranes of the heart get stronger, as do the veins and arteries; dormant capillaries open up in the muscle, resulting in many more being available to meet the workload. Only at this point, together with other factors, do we have a correspondingly greater and more efficient uptake of oxygen throughout the body. We refer to this system as the cardio-vascular system which becomes much more efficient with exercise.

Flexibility and stretching exercises, particularly as part of the Warm-up Procedures, are most important, both to increase the range of movement and to stretch the parts which are to be used in the activity programme. They must be carried out in a slow and controlled manner throughout. These are the areas of importance for swimming:

1. Gastrocs and soleous stretch; hamstrings; quadriceps; hip adductors; adductors lumbar extensors; abdominals.
2. Trunk side flexors; trapezius; shoulder stretch pectorals; neck extensors.

The Warm-up

The warm-up is an integral part of training; conducted thoroughly, it increases the body temperature and ensures that sufficient quantities of blood are delivered to the exercising muscles. This in turn ensures that an abundant number of capillaries open up so the oxygen supply from the blood is increased, and faster nerve impulses will also be accomplished. In water, the warm-up should consist of swimming the first few lengths as slowly as possible, then building to a comfortable speed.

At the end of a vigorous pool session a 'swim-down' must take place. This ensures that an adequate amount of blood returns to the heart, which assists the removal of lactic acid and other waste products.

DIET AND NUTRITION ――――――

The ability to train to the levels which could ensure success in top competition may be considerably affected by the swimmer's diet. A healthy diet is one that provides for the energy we need in training requirements. Energy is made up from three basic nutrients: carbohydrates, proteins and fats. Carbohydrates are broken down and stored as glycogen; most is stored in the muscle, although some is stored in the liver. Fat is stored in the adipose tissue and muscle cells. Swimmers who eat sensibly should get all the vitamins, proteins and minerals they need from any food intake. At 'steady state' training (aerobic), both fat and carbohydrate will provide for energy requirements. As exercise becomes more intense, the swimmer will rely more on carbohydrate and less fat is used. When exercising is higher than 50 per cent VO_2 max, the energy in fat cannot be released quickly enough; at approximately 60 per cent, the contributions of fat and carbohydrate are about equal, but above this figure the contribution to energy requirements is carbohydrate. The body cannot store vast amounts of carbohydrate; the muscles store it in the form of glycogen and these amounts are small, with the result that between sixty to ninety minutes of intensive training can use up most of it – and depletion leads to fatigue. Moreover once glycogen levels are depleted these can only be replaced at about 5 per cent per hour, and it takes almost a full day to replace all full stocks. It is sensible therefore to eat as quickly as possible (in small amounts) after competition.

If the swimmer has the wrong intake of food levels, he or she will reach a stage of being unable to cope, or of 'falling adaptation'. When training, a high carbohydrate drink is one way of 'refuelling'. If the water is too warm in any training session (by which I mean a figure of 83° plus), then a swimmer can dehydrate in water. Fluid intake is important even in the training environment of swimming.

At times too much emphasis can be placed upon the diet, and a well balanced diet is usually found from 'normal' eating habits. Olga Brusnikina, the fourteen-year-old Russian sensation to synchro, won the Junior World Championship in Leeds in 1993. She was asked, 'What kind of food do you eat as part of your nutritional programme?' She replied, 'Anything that's in the fridge.'

10
Weight Training

Strength is an important consideration in any programme and is basically why men are faster than women. When contemplating any weight programme, there are certain things you must always take into account:

• Young swimmers should not be part of the programme until they have finished growing.

• Machine weights are far safer than loose weights but you will get less in the ranges of movement.

• Deep breathing is an important concept in the movement of weights.

• Tracksuits and good footwear must always be worn in the weight-training room: non-slip shoes, no bare feet, and no rings as they tend to get damaged.

• Under-estimate load and volume and only then gradually increase.

• Check all equipment and floorspace before starting.

• Limited equipment and the need for 'spotters' on some exercises generally indicates a team of three, one lifting and two 'spotting'.

• The correct methods of lifting weights must be taught and insisted upon.

Keeping good form throughout is the safe way to train.

The following definitions may also be helpful: **Strength** is the force output of the musculo-skeletal system, measured by one maximal contraction, ideally a dynomometer. **Power** is the rate of working force × velocity, ie muscle strength and limb velocity. In more practical terms, consider the observation made by Andy Kerr, BAWLA senior coach and UK power-lifting champion: 'If a labourer works with a 5lb shovel, he will work happily all day. If the shovel is exchanged for a larger one, then he will experience stress until the muscles relate to the heavier load'. Any weight programme observes a similar concept. Moreover, very often a swimmer has strong legs and weak arms or vice versa, so the individual programme should be structured to give extra work to the weaker muscle groups.

A WEIGHT-TRAINING PROGRAMME RELATING TO SPEED

This will comprise two or three sets of five to ten repetitions of heavy weights. Once the swimmer can manage the multiples in both weight and repetitions

Weight-Training Variables

	High	*Medium*	*Low*
Sessions per week	Daily plus weight-lifting 3/5 power-lifting 3/4 thrower off-season	2/3 Most sports off-season 2/3 thrower in season	1-Low power sports 1/2 in season Training most sports
Selection of *Exercises (No.)*	Bodybuilding 10+ Novices Off season training	6/8 Average for most programmes	Power lifting 5 or less. Specialized training and advanced training in certain sports. Reduced time situations
Number of sets per exercise	5+ Lifting sports. Advanced trainers in high power sports	3/4 Most forms of general weight-training, majority of time	1/2 Novices 1/2 periods when time or energy are short
No. of reps per set	10+ Fitness for local muscular endurance	5/8 most types of training for most sports	1/4 for maximum strength and power much of a lifter's training
Resistance % of Maximum	Over 80%	Between 60% and 80%	Up to 60%
Speed of movement	Weight-lifting Advanced power training	Will depend on the exercises, general aim – fast with good technique	Bodybuilding. Novices – learning new techniques and loosening up
Rest intervals between sets	Power-lifting and heavy power training – over 3 minutes	Normal training – 1½/3 mins	General fitness – less than 90 secs

successfully, the weight can be increased by a small amount. Initially the swimmer might fail in the number of repetitions, but before long he should be able to cope. When he does, the weight is again increased.

A WEIGHT-TRAINING PROGRAMME RELATING TO ENDURANCE ─────

This programme entails two or three sets of an adequate number of repetitions with lighter weights, say thirty to forty repetitions of 14–18kg in weight. When the swimmer is proficient with these, the sets remain the same but the repetitions are increased. The swimmer will have to adapt the weight to suit individual comparisons. The repetitions and sets are the important factors.

SEASONAL WEIGHT-TRAINING PLANNING ─────

Some sports have a straight season, for example football, cricket, hockey and rugby. Other sports have a season with a structured programme of major contests, for example athletics has national championships and trials, followed by the more important international events. Weight-lifting, power-lifting and other sports go on all the year round and the timing of a championship or a major competition will depend entirely on the standard and aims of the individual.

Straight Season

In this programme there is no peak for any one contest.

Closed season: Three times a week ie Monday, Wednesday, Friday. High number of exercises, low number of sets, high repetitions: Fitness – endurance – learning.

Pre-season: Three times a week. Reduce the exercises and repetitions, increase the resistance and sets: Strength and Power.

Start of the season: Twice a week ie Monday, Wednesday. Reduce the exercises and repetitions. Increase the resistance: Increasing power but saving in time and energy.

Throughout the season: Twice a week. Increase the repetitions and reduce the resistance a little: Maintenance.

WEIGHT TRAINING FOR SWIMMING –

Exercises for starts, turns and stroke leg action include half squats; jump squats; leg presses; and the hack lift.

Half squats: Swimmers should try to maintain an upright trunk and hip-width foot spacing. If you need to save time in a

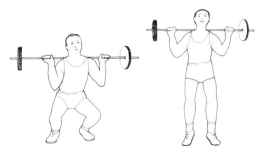

Fig 53 Half squats.

session, squats can be combined with a calf raise onto the toes (heavier weights can be used).

Fig 54   Jump squats.

Jump squats: These strengthen the trunk, hip, leg and ankle extensors; it is a dynamic exercise. It is of course necessary to check the balance between each landing and take-off.

Leg press: The pressure must be taken by the pelvis, and not by the lumbar vertebrae. This exercise can be combined with

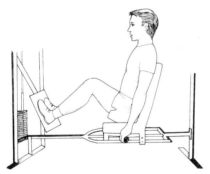

Fig 55   Leg press.

Fig 56   The back lift.

a toe press to strengthen the plantar-flexors.

The hack lift: The heels are positioned on a block of wood with the barbell positioned behind the legs. Squat down with the body erect, then rise until the legs are straight.

WEIGHT-TRAINING EXERCISES FOR THE DIFFERENT STROKES

Front Crawl: Upper Body Exercises

Recovery:	Single arm rowing. Alternate dumbbell press.
Forward and backward scull:	Bent over stroke simulations. Alternate barbell exercise.

Backstroke: Upper Body Exercises

Recovery:	Supine alternate dumbbell raise.
Entry and pull phase:	Pull-downs behind the neck; 'over-grip' (lats)
Pull and push phase:	Bench dips (safe/stable bench, triceps); bench press.

Butterfly: Upper Body Exercises

Recovery:	Standing lateral raise; bent over rowing.
Catch and pull phase:	Bench press; pull-downs in front. May be combined in one long 'pull/push' movement 'over-grip'.
Push phase:	Triceps push downwards.

Breaststroke: Upper Body Exercises

Recovery: Narrow grip standing press.

Outsweep/ insweep: Pull-downs in front; bench press; dumbbell simulations (body horizontal, narrow bench).

Trunk Exercises

These provide stability.

Abdominals: Bent knees help to eliminate back problems. Remember that the range of movement of the spinal flexors is small: do not be misled by the impressive range of movement of the hip joint. Twisting and side-bend movements are necessary to work the oblique, as well as the longitudinal range of abdominal muscles. Extensor muscles can be worked by prone hyper-extensions and floor back-bridge.

SCHEDULE CONSTRUCTION ——

Select eight to ten exercises covering all the major muscle groups; for example:

Pull-downs in the front:

Fig 57.

Standing triceps press:
To develop the muscles at the rear of the upper arm.

Fig 58.

Sideways lateral raise:
To develop the shoulder and upper back muscles.

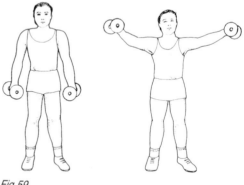

Fig 59.

Supine straight-arm pull-overs:
To enlarge the thorax and develop the muscles surrounding the shoulder girdle,

Fig 60.

the muscles on the front of the chest and the large muscles of the lower back.

Pull-down to the neck:

To develop the upper back muscles of the shoulder and those at the rear of the upper arm.

Fig 61.

Single-arm rowing:

Bend over from the waist. Hold a dumb-bell in one hand; the other holds the bench for support. Extend ahead, tracing a sculling path that relates to the swimming stroke. Press backwards and repeat the exercise. The stroke simulation will develop the upper back muscles, the trunk, and the muscles on the front and

Fig 62.

side of the upper arm. On a long push through it will develop the muscles at the rear of the upper arm.

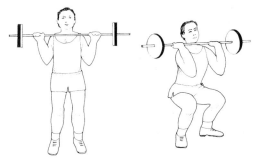

Fig 63.

Half-squat raise:

This develops the muscles of the hips and the buttocks, the front of the thighs and the calf muscles.

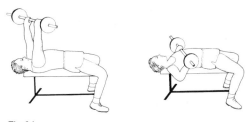

Fig 64.

Bench press:

To develop the chest muscles, the front of the shoulder muscles and the muscles on the back of the upper arm.

Fig 65.

Sit-ups with alternate twists

Repetitions

Bearing in mind that endurance can be

gained in the water with over-distance, aim for strength and power with ten or fifteen repetitions.

Sets:	The first session should comprise one set each, then gradually increase to three or four.
Weights:	Start with an underload (too light a weight), then increase as confidence and competence grows.

Individuals who are not fit at all should be given an even lower repetition to bring them to the required strength levels for swimming, then the repetitions can be increased. Not all the exercises require the same emphasis; for example, power phase exercises can be three to five sets, and recovery phase exercises perhaps only one to two sets.

PREPARATION FOR A MAJOR CONTEST

It is humanly impossible to progress with constantly rising achievements. Nevertheless, training methods have advanced enormously in the last twenty years and have been the major factor in the general rise in standards.

Principle Stage of Preparation

Basic conditioning phase:	To develop fitness, endurance and changes in technique (3 to 6 weeks).
Preparation phase:	Development of specific qualities required for the event (4 to 8 weeks).
Competition phase:	Higher quality work, lower volume (4 to 8 weeks).
Final week:	Last weight training well into competitive stage of competition. A period of recovery with again a lower volume of work. It is important not to do the best performance in training.
Post-contest:	A period of active rest, allowing for mental and physical recovery (1 to 4 weeks).

The Pulse Rate as a Measure of Stress and Recovery

The banal (at rest) pulse rate will vary between individuals. As a guide, the pulse rate of a swimmer in good shape will be in the region of fifty to sixty beats per minute. In these days of scientific advances, the pulse rate to assess stress and recovery is used as a guide only, although in training situations it is useful. After a severe workload it can climb to about 200 P.P.M.; after one minute, however, it should have fallen to 120–140. The fitter the individual, the faster the pulse rate will fall and the better the recovery rate.

'Swimming down' is important after a vigorous set, for this reason: working muscle groups assist the flow of blood back to the heart, but this action ceases when work stops and then 'blood pooling' will occur; 'swimming-down' reinstates the flow back to the heart. Take the pulse count as soon as the activity ceases: place the middle finger over the carotid artery in the neck, count the beats over six seconds, then add a nought to estimate the pulse rate for one minute.

TRAINING APPLIED: A SUMMARY ——

We have already discussed how the body adapts to its oxygen requirements. The coach must now work out practical methods to bring about the physiological changes which are necessary if the swimmer is to succeed at the highest competitive levels. There are only three methods of training, and they are:

Under load
distance training
(aerobic)

Pressed load
(aerobic and
anaerobic)

Overload
speed training
(anaerobic)

Fig 66.

In order for the above three methods to be successful, we must devise a system of work and then use a formula which will achieve our requirements. Swimming coaches will often put together a programme of work in the water and blandly refer to it as a 'schedule' (See Chapter 11 for Schedule Compilation); but any schedule, and particularly one from a well used source, must be adjusted to suit both the period and the requirements of the individual. The creative coach will fashion the schedule to attain individual targets, thereby moulding the talented swimmer into a talented champion. Compose the schedule to bring about the necessary physiological changes, know your subject and think in depth: then the rewards are deeply satisfying.

11

Schedule Compilation

If a number of coaches were asked to formulate a schedule for a particular swimmer for the same period of the season, they would all differ in some way or another, an indication of their individual outlook. It must be freely admitted that the swimming coach is entrenched in one of the most boring training environments, so it is imperative that he keeps both body and mind in overdrive throughout the programme. An imaginative, challenging schedule with the motivating initiative of a good coach behind it engenders respect from all concerned. All good age group and senior swimmers appreciate a hard session, so the coach should always make his programme stimulating with a varied sequence at each session.

Sometimes a schedule doesn't work, so he must be ready to change it accordingly. Most coaches will prepare their schedule in advance which is a good policy but nevertheless it must be based on a cyclical routine or the time of year and on the prevalent weaknesses of the swimmers. Not many coaches plan a session to its very last moment, so they 'overload' it accordingly. Chapter 9 refers to the principles of training where the annual plan has three phases in the year. The coach must now:

- Work to a plan.

- Gauge the type of schedule.
- Analyse what is required, and then make provision in the schedule for it; for example it must accommodate the general faults apparent in the swimmers, inferior techniques in stroke (it could be butterfly), starts and turns.

Presentation methods vary from one coach to another: some write up the whole session, others reveal it one section at a time. It all comes down to the individuality of the coach.

WRITING A SCHEDULE

Basically, all coaches use the same shorthand version of writing a schedule, and the rules for this should not create too much of a problem:

a. Keep it short and simple.

b. All swimmers know that the pool is measured in yards or metres, so there is no need to refer to this.

c. Refer to the following in a shortened form:
The strokes as F/C – B/C – brst – Fly
A distance that is repeated as 5×100 F/C
A distance set that is repeated as $3 \times 5 \times 100$ F/C

Warm-up and swim-down as W/U and S/D
A controlled breathing sequence would be written as:

4 × 100 F/C hypoxic 5 on 1.45 – purge swim 50/100
4 × 100 F/C hypoxic 7 on 1.50 – purge swim 50/100
4 × 100 F/C hypoxic 9 on 2 mins – purge swim 50/100

A swimmer will relate more to arm pulls (half stroke cycle) than one complete stroke cycle, in stroke counting sets.

Swim Time and Intervals of Rest

If an interval of rest is added in the swim set, this may appear to suit all criteria for the set:

10 × 100 F/C RI 20

However, this places no obligation on the swimmer to swim fast, so each 100m could be swum as slowly as he desired. But if we add an 'on time' instead of a 'rest interval', the swimmer must now achieve a time for the swim, regardless of rest in the stipulated 'on time':

10 × 100 F/C 'on' 1.45

This still may not achieve the 'overload' factor desired by the coach. A swim for 100m in 1 min 35 secs with a rest interval of 10 secs could be an easy swim for many; but if we include a target time in that swim, then we get somewhere near our requirements:

10 × 100 F/C on 1.45 T.T. 1.20 (target time)

The last example would be good for a group of swimmers but still would not 'target' the individual swimmer. You can achieve this by the inclusion of a 'percentage' time factor based on the individual swimmer's competitive best time, as in example 'a'. This swim may have to use percentage tables because some swimmers are simply not fast enough in working out their percentages, and time in water is a valuable commodity. A far easier method is to add a time factor, as in example 'b', and it also approximates with 'percentage swims':

a. 10 × 100 F/C on 1.45 - 25% + P.B. (Personal Best Time 60 secs) = T.T. 1 min 15 secs
b. 10 × 100 F/C on 1.45 T.T. P.B + 15 secs

How to Gauge Your Type of Schedule

• If you include plenty of kicking and pulling, then you will cover less distance.

• It will depend on the time of the year.

• A 'distance' schedule will have more yardage. A 'speed' schedule will have less yardage.

• The more sections the longer the explanation time, and therefore the less distance will be covered. A five-sectional schedule will have approximately 8 mins of 'dead' time and so only 52 mins of work. A mixed schedule is one that includes a variety of work with swims and can be chosen from the following:

Front crawl with back crawl
Medley section
Sectional swims (kicking and pulling)
No 1 or 'A' stroke
Starts and turn techniques
Sprints

Distance will include front crawl with back crawl only. Plan the schedules one week at a time. The following percentages are important:

Preparatory period

40% front crawl and/or back crawl
25% individual medley
15% sectional work (kicking, pulling, starts and turns)
15% No 1 stroke ('A' stroke)
5% sprints or technique 'wave swims'

Pre-Competitive Period

The weekly yardage will have decreased slightly.

30% front crawl or back crawl
25% individual medley
20% sectional work (kicking, pulling, starts and turns)
20% No 1 stroke
5% sprints

Competitive Period

The weekly yardage drops still further, so try for more hours, especially in the morning.

25% front crawl and/or back crawl
20% individual medley
25% 'A' sectional with starts and turns
25% No 1 stroke
5% sprints, but most other swims will have an emphasis on quality work

Technique must be developed at an early age, but coach, and don't pressurize the less able swimmer. Develop the aerobic capacity and the ability of a swimmer to swim longer distances at an early stage: 500m to a 1,000m warm-up swims; 400m to 800m time trials. Train as often as possible, because success comes from the dedication of both swimmer and coach.

The first part of the schedule must be the warm-up, with a distance of at least 400m or more depending on your water time. The next part of the schedule is the 'main section', the portion in which 'over-load' should be achieved. In this main section the coach will employ different types of training swim to achieve his targets. These can also be used in other sections of the schedule by working out different swim formations. In this way not only are defined targets achieved but the schedules are kept interesting with the different presentations. The difference will be in the swimmer's general attitude to training; instead of I'm not looking forward to training, he will think 'I wonder what the coach has got for us this session'. The change from apathy to interest lies with creative thinking and a few strokes with a piece of chalk.

TYPES OF TRAINING SWIM

Fartlek Swims

(Preparation or pre-competitive.) Known as 'aerobic threshold', this was a type of training routine in Scandinavia. Zatopek, the great Hungarian runner, demolished other competitors using its concept in over-distance athletic events. It consists of swimming over distance with a varying speed ingredient, but never reaching exhaustion levels:

$$5 \times \frac{200 \text{ F/C RI 20}}{4 \times 50 \text{ F/C on 45}}$$

The set of 50s can be altered for a longer rest, but with a target time swim eg 4 x 50 on 60 secs T.T. 30 secs.

Fartlek 2 × 900 F/C RI 60 (ladder swim 6 × 150)

The ladder swim means that each of the six swimmers in the lane leads for 150m – 100m slow and 50m sprint – going to the back of the group of swimmers after his turn; each swimmer therefore shares the workload.

Over-distance Swims

(Preparation period; aerobic.) This involves swimming greater distances at a slower pace. It achieves cardio-vascular and muscular endurance with a build-up of fitness, technique and confidence.

5 × 400 F/C on 5.45

Slow Interval Training

(Early pre-competitive; aerobic.) This involves the use of middle-distance sets for the build-up of cardio-vascular endurance, very similar to those in the over-distance swims except that target times may now be adapted into the swims.

5 × 400 F/C on 5.45/6 mins T.T.
5.15/5.30

Controlled Interval Training

(Pre-competitive and competitive.) This training is based on the **D**istance swum – the **I**nterval of rest – the **R**epetitions of the repeat swims – and the **T**ime taken to swim the distance: DIRT.

Fast Interval Training

(Competitive and taper; anaerobic.) Again using the DIRT principle, it is 'partial recovery' training, otherwise known as anaerobic (oxygen debt) with a build-up of lactic acid in the muscle. This type of training helps the swimmer to tolerate pain and related stress as encountered in speed training.

8 × 100 F/C on 2.15 and hold T.T. P.B. + 8/10 secs

Sprint Training

(Competitive and taper; anaerobic.) This uses short distances, faster than race pace with long rests and acclimatizes the swimmer to sprints by improving the techniques he must use in competitive events. It also gives basic speed.

Repetition Swims

(Taper period; anaerobic.) This is faster than race pace, but less than the race distance. Long rests with a recovery pulse rate.

a. 6 × 75 F/C on 2.30, pulse rate recovery low region
b. 6 × 50 F/C on 1.45/2 mins, pulse rate recovery low region

Locomotive Swims

(Preparation/pre-competitive.) There is a similarity between these swims and the Fartlek type of training sets. The locomotive swim comprises a fast swim with an 'active rest' swim, and is set over distances to test the concentration and the disciplinary powers of the swimmer:

a. F/C 25 fast, 25 slow – 50 fast, 50 slow – 75 fast, 75 slow
100 fast, 100 slow – 125 fast, 125 slow

b. If combined with a Hungarian sequence:
F/C 25 fast, 25 slow – 50 fast, 50 slow
75 fast, 75 slow – 100 fast, 100 slow
125 fast, 125 slow – 150 fast, 150 slow
100 fast, 100 slow – 75 fast, 75 slow
50 fast, 50 slow – 25 fast, 25 slow

c. If combined with an 'A' stroke, eg Fly, each sectional distance of the locomotive is done half on the 'A' stroke and half on F/C:
Fly 25 fast, 25 slow – 50 fast Fly, 50 slow F/C
Alt Fly, F/C up to the desired distance and then back down

Mixed or Straight Lane Swims

(Preparation/pre-competitive.) The aim is to develop strength and endurance. To start the set half the swimmers take up position in lane 1 and half in lane 6 (if a six-lane pool). They swim butterfly up the lane they are in, turn under the lane rope and swim F/C down the next lane; they then turn under the next lane rope and swim up the next lane with butterfly. The first swimmer having swum three lengths now crosses under the two lane ropes back to lane 1 or 6 and starts again. This set gives freedom and room, especially for the butterfly stroke. The 'A' stroke can be brought into the set as required.

THE COMPONENTS FOR TYPES OF SWIM

Link Swims

These are used to establish 'race pace'. This must be worked upon, especially with the distance swimmer.

In the following examples, a. is for the sprint swimmer and b. is for the distance swimmer.

   a. 6 × 25m F/C on 50 T.T. 15 secs
   b. 6 × 50m F/C on 90 T.T. 30 secs

The target time for the swimmer for the forthcoming competition could be 60 secs. The interval of rest between sets would be a 'talk-back' between swimmer and coach.

Broken Repetitions

Each swim would have a short rest, eg 10 secs. This would be long enough for the swimmer to take his time off the pace clock, and readjust the swim accordingly:

   5 × 100 F/C broken at 50 for 10 on 2 mins T.T. 32 secs

High Quality Repetitionds

These repetitions are swum over the race distance with a long rest:

   5 × 100 F/C on 3 mins T.T. 60 secs

The rest interval may even be a 'talk-back'.

Time Trials

These trials are used as a measure of progress and also in the 'challenge' situation for team selection. However, they must be used with care because they may have a demoralizing effect on the losing swimmer.

Straight Sets

Here, the distance and rest intervals remain constant:

   3 × 6 × 100 F/C on 1.45

Mixed Sets

The distances and rest intervals differ; usually the distances decrease in length.

   2 × 400 F/C on 5.30 – 4 × 200 F/C on 3 mins – 6 × 100 F/C on 90

Descending/Reducing and Progressive Sets

The aim of these sets is to increase the pace of each succeeding repetition.

   a. 4 × 100 F/C on 90 T.T 1.10 – 4 × 100 F/C on 1.45 T.T. 68/69
   4 × 100 F/C on
   2 mins T.T. 66/67
   b. It could also be written as:
   3 × 4 × 100 F/C on 90 – 1.45/2 mins hold and descend by 2 secs on each set

Hungarian Sets

Apparently these sets came from the training ideas of the Hungarian water polo coaches. The distances and rest intervals change in each succeeding set. They create interest for the swimmers, and the coach can make use of other components to give an even greater challenge.

a. 6 × 25 F/C on 40
    6 × 50 F/C on 50
    4 × 100 F/C on 90
    1 × 400 F/C on 5.45
    4 × 100 F/C on 90
    6 × 50 F/C on 50
    6 × 25 F/C on 40
b. 6 × 25 F/C on 40 T.T. 13
    6 × 50 F/C on 50 T.T. 30
    4 × 100 F/C on 90 T.T 1.15
    1 × 400 F/C on 90 T.T 5.15
    4 × 100 F/C on 80
    6 × 50 F/C on 45
    6 × 25 F/C on 40

The target times in the second set can be added to the sets to create greater overload and interest. The Hungarian routines can also be used in sectional and individual medley workouts.

Negative Splits

This is a routine in which the second half of the race is swum faster than the first half.

a. 4 × 100 F/C push-offs, 1st 50 30 secs, 2nd 50 29 secs
b. 3 × 100 F/C dive starts, 1st 50 T.T. 28 secs, 2nd 50 T.T. 29/30 secs (where you allow 1.5/2 secs for the dive start)

Race Simulator

These are similar to the broken repetitions swims, but are much harder as the speed ingredient is greater.

4 × 100 F/C broken at 50 for 10 on 4 mins T.T. 27/28 secs

Equate the types, components and methods for achieving the swim targets, in order to build your schedule for the required period in the year.

INTEGRATION FACTORS IN THE SCHEDULE

- The factors to be considered.
- The number of swimmers involved.
- The age and sex of the swimmers.
- The ability levels.
- General considerations at the start of training.
- Events and distances for which the swimmers are aiming.

INCLUSIVE ANNUAL FACTORS OF THE SCHEDULES

- The time of year or peak phase.
- The warm-up.
- The main section; don't include too much variety: the work must be meaningful and produce what is intended.
- Sectional work.
- Starts and turns (not always to be included).
- Short sprint work.
- Swim-down.

You should aim for 2,800m to 3,000m swimming distance to be covered for each hour of the schedule, depending on the time of the year and your calibre of swimmer.

DISTANCE SWIMS

A distance set of repeat swims is primarily

Average Swim Times and Maximum Numbers of Swimmers in a Lane

25m pool, average swim time 20/22 secs; 5/6 maximum per lane.

33⅓m pool, average swim time 25 secs; 7/8 maximum per lane.

50m pool, average swim time 40 secs; 10/12 maximum per lane.

meant to develop a base for fitness and endurance, with a good level of cardio-vascular efficiency. As we have discussed, energy is produced by ATP in the muscle fibres and is the result of aerobic and anaerobic work rates (see Chapter 9, 'Principles of Training'). In distance swim sets, we work on the aerobic pathway because this creates a capacity for the oxy-dization of carbohydrate and fats which results in the production of energy. Distance work consists of over-distance swims or sets, usually from 200m to 1,000m and even longer distances with short intervals of rest. It is the prime ingre-dient for the main section of the schedule in the preparation period of your annual plan. The changes that are brought about in the muscles by aerobic training are as follows:

1. An increase in the number of mitochrondria (a portion of the cell which contains enzymes involved in the aerobic production of energy).
2. Increased O_2 storage in the muscle (myoglobin).
3. An increase in the fibre diameter.
4. An increase in the number of capil-liaries in the muscle.

Cardio-vascular changes brought about by aerobic training include:

1. An increase in the thickness of the heart muscle, and an increase in the diameter of the heart chambers.

2. An increased stroke volume.
3. A decrease in the heart rate.
4. A lowering of the blood pressure.

Over-distance work is vital, but it can be boring so it is up to the creative ability of the coach to make this part of the pro-gramme both challenging and interest-ing. He can do this by coaching his swim-mers in the following routines:

• Swimming at a given time factor and pulse rate.
• Learning to swim at a given pace.
• And having accomplished a given pace, sustaining and holding that pace over a set of repeat swims.

Coaches should beware of the over-distance set with a constant interval of rest. Although necessary early in the preparation period when the swimmer is unfit, our objective is always to attain sub-maximal work rates by means of pro-gressive overload. In order to achieve this, we must inject a speed ingredient after the level of fitness has been attained. Lesser distances are also a necessary com-ponent in the sets. The progressive steps and the factors that might be used could be:

Initial period of fitness
5 × 200 F/C on 2.40/3 mins, hold average swim times

5 × 400 F/C on 5.30/6 mins, hold aver-age swim time throughout

To improve upon a level of attained fitness

5 × 200 F/C on 2.40/3 mins hold 1 and 2; descend by 2 secs and hold for 3/4 and 5

5 × 400 F/C on 5.30/6 mins; hold all swim times

To learn a given pace

5 × 200 F/C on 2.45/3.10, 1 and 2 broken at 100 for 10 secs, 3/4 and 5 hold broken 100 times × 2

5 × 400 F/C as above 200s example. Hold 400 pace on an 800 swim

Obviously the major objective for the over-distance swimmer is a high level of fitness, endurance and pace. Once fitness and endurance are established, then a speed criterion built up to a level of race pace should be the objective. The following examples of schedules encompassing all the necessary criteria may be used and adapted to suit individual requirements.

STRAIGHT SETS ——————

(Preparation period)

1. 600 F/C (loosen and bilateral) and 200 B/C W/U
2. Swim half-hour continuous F/C
3. Kick 6 × 100 'A' RI 20, pull 4 × 200 'A' RI 20 on Fly alternating 1 length Fly and 1 F/C
4. Starts and technique swims

1. 10 mins flexibility, then 1 × 600 F/C and 200 B/C W/U
2. 3 × alternate 400 and 200 F/C on 5.30 and 2.45
3. Kick 3 × alternate 150 and 100 'A' RI 20
   Pull 'A', either 3 × 300 F/C, 4 × 200 B/C or 3 × 150 Brst/Fly
   Swim 'A' 3 × 400 F/C, B/C or 5 × 200

Brst/Fly RI 30
4. Turns 10 mins

1.5hrs schedule, distance approx 4,200m.

1. 800 F/C (bilateral and loosen) and B/C W/U with drills
   2. 3 × 3 × 200
   F/C or Alt F/C, B/C – 1st set RI 30 – 2nd RI 20 – 3rd RI 10 shirts and paddles
3. Pull 3 × 400 F/C RI 20 shirts and paddles
   Kick 6 × 100 'A' RI descending from 30 to 10 secs
   Swim 400s on F/C and B/C and 150s on Brst/Fly technique swims RI 30
4. Relay take-overs

1. 10 mins flexibility, then W/U swim 600 F/C
2. 3 × 900 F/C Fartlek ladder swim; each 900 is 100 easy with 50 hard RI 60 between 900s
3. Pull 400s F/C or B/C with 150s for Brst and Fly RI 20
   Kick alternating 200s and 100s RI 20
   Swim 3 × 400 F/C or 3 × 300 B/C; Brst/Fly 3 × 150 RI 20
4. 'Pike' starts 10 mins

1.5 hours schedule, distance approx 4,500/5,000m.

Swimming sets can now include the use of shirt or tube and paddles. Fly routines can alternate with 'break-up' lengths of front crawl; these will help to establish a good level of technique. The coach must decide on a weight programme suitable for distance work and the time of the year; he must also decide at what phase and with what routines he will commence work for the sprint swimmer. Land conditioning should include circuits and flexibility work, with flexibility work before *all* swim sessions.

Preparation Period

(Lipid Metabolism: Heart-rate zone 60%; maximum heart rate 140, with 60 mins duration)

1. W/U 800 O/C (own choice) F/C or B/C
2. Swim 2 × 800 F/C RI 15
3. Pull 400 F/C timed swim breathe 5
    Kick straight 600 without boards
    Swim 400 F/C or B/C or 200 Brst/Fly then 20 × 50 on 60/70 'A'
4. 15 min starts

1. 800 F/C W/U
2. 2 × 8 × 100 F/C 2nd set hypoxic 5 and 7 on 1.45
3. Kick 6 × 100 'A' without boards
    Pull 4 × 300 F/C or B/C or 3 × 150 Brs/Fly RI work
    Swim an 800 set of 'A' alternating 200s and 4 × 50 on 60
4. 15 mins turns

Approximately 4,800m with starts and turns.

The work in the next phase will become harder and more demanding, so this is the time to make stroke changes. Ensure that any changes are rigidly enforced and that improvements are made now. Start and turn techniques must be understood by both coach and swimmer, from tumble to flip turns and grab to pike starts. Coach the front crawl throw-away turn first because then it is easier to progress to the breast and fly turn techniques, with emphasis on the fall-away and pull-up phases. Work on techniques too, using films and videos. Finally hypoxic routines should now be established in the sets.

Late Preparatory Phase

(Anaerobic threshold)

1. 800 F/C broken at 400 for 15

2. 2 × 200 F/C RI 20/10; 3 × 5 × 50 F/C RI 20; 15 and 10 shirts and paddles up to 2nd set of 5 × 50s (H.P.R. 170/180)
3. 'A' stroke Pull 400 F/C easy pull 8 × 50 on 70/1.30 descending in sets of 2
    Hungarian kick: 3 × 100 on 2.30 T.T. 1.45
    4 × 50 on 80 looking for hold at 45/50
    3 × 100 decreasing pace
4. Push-off swim sprints and swim-downs

1.5 hour schedule, approximately 4,000m.

1. 800 active stretching and technique W/U
2. 3 × 4 × 100 F/C hypoxic on 5, 7 and 9, each set on 1.40 1.50 and 2 mins
3. 600 paddle pull F/C then 6 × 100 'A' pull
    Kick 6 × 100 'A' on 2.30 T.T. hold 1.45
    Swim descending 100 sets (an.thr.)
4. 15 mins starts and turns, whichever is weaker

A level of fitness can now be said to have been established. Pace and speed are injected into the schedules with anaerobic threshold sets, and these swims are timed to ensure that targets are met and held. Fitness work still includes land conditioning, with heavier weights brought in for the sprint swimmers.

HYPOXIC SWIMS ———

Hypoxic or 'controlled methods' of swim training are employed to create a high level of oxygen debt with less intensive work levels. At these levels of work it is also possible to hold the techniques associated with each stroke. Obviously there is less oxygen available to both the working body and muscle groups, and the lungs must now extract all the inspired oxygen possible; thus the intra-cellular capacity of individual cells must be made more efficient. Oxygen is delivered by an improved level of red blood cells, and is used more efficiently. If used logically, hypoxic training is extremely beneficial; it is also claimed to have the following advantages:

1. It increases the muscles' ability to create ATP with a proportional increase in the number of mitochondria, including enzymes and co-enzymes.
2. There is a possible increase in the amount of glycogen stored in the muscles.
3. There is an increase in the enzymes which permit the release of ATP in the lactic acid–ATP system.
(Counsilman 1974 ASCA clinic.)

Methods of training involving controlled breathing should be used with both logic and care, conducted at a slower speed with controlled pace. Whether the breathing cycle is odd or even will depend on the swimmer being unilateral or bilateral. Over the shorter distances the swimmer will be able to breathe less for more stroke cycles, with a higher ratio over the longer distances. This type of training is usually only associated with front crawl, but it should also be included in and relate to the other three strokes. It has been found (through practical experience) that excessive controlled breathing work can create headaches; however, if a 'purge' (normal breathing) swim is included with the hypoxic workout then headaches will not occur.

If we consider that a swimmer can be out of oxygen for anything up to three or four seconds (I/M back-to-breast turn, racing starts etc), then it may be said that hypoxic training is imperative as a method of preparing the body for race conditions. Hypoxic work should be maintained throughout the full training curriculum; examples of hypoxic routines could be as follows:

1. 1×800 F/C 1st 200 slow; 2nd alt catch-up 1 length and normal; 3rd pull-up turns; 4th bilateral
2. 4×100 F/C on 1.40 hypoxic 3
    4×100 F/C on 1.50 hypoxic 5 with 100 purge swim
    4×100 F/C on 2 mins hypoxic 7 with 100 purge swim
    or 3×400 F/C on 5.45/6.15 hypoxic 5 with purge swims

This can be broken up with alternating sets of one length hypoxic 5 and one breathing normal – 50s hypoxic and normal – 100s hypoxic with a 50 purge/normal swim. The computations are many. One way that controlled breathing sets are particularly good is in a race preparation set, for example:

'Side and kick turn set' race simulation with controlled pace; pre-competitive, competitive or taper period.

The start: The swimmer can push off from the wall into the swim or, better still, lie horizontally in the water holding the wall, rail or scum trough. A slight alternating leg action will maintain the body position. A 'throw-away' turn with the body 'knifing' away from the wall will establish the start and the necessary depth. The 'throw-away' turn orientates the body and helps it to maintain a side elevation in all tumble-turn techniques.

Transition into the swim: four to six kicks and two to three pulls into the swim without breathing, then normal breathing.

The turn: three to four kicks away from the wall and two pulls without breathing, then normal breathing.

The finish: As soon as the lane 'tee' marker (pool bottom) is seen, swim into the wall without breathing.

The sets can comprise 50s or 100s front crawl with the appropriate rest equating to the pace of the swim. Hypoxic or controlled breathing training is invaluable for transition to the above sets, although it can take up to six months to establish a comfortable relationship for the swimmer.

Early Pre-Competitive

(Anaerobic, with An threshold)

1. 400 F/C and 200 B/C, pulse rates 140
2. 3 × 10 × 50 F/C RI 20/15/10 secs hold swim times
3. 900 alternating lanes swim, Fly and F/C (6 × 150) shirts on first 600. (Pulse rate RI from 180 to 150/160) between 150s
4. 'A' stroke: kick 5 × 100 on 2.30 T.T. 140 Pull 200s for B/C and F/C and 150s for Brst/Fly on 3.20 Swim a descending set of 3 × 5 × 50 on 60/70
5. Ones technique, swims at 80% effort

1. 800 F/C 200 slow; 200 alt catch-up and sliding crawl; 200 bilateral and 200 long sliding crawl
2. 3 × 3 × 100 F/C hypoxic work on 140 – 150 and 2 mins breathe 3 – 5 and 7 on sets. 100 purge swim between sets
3. 'A' pull, kick, swim - 3 × 3 × ... 200s B/C and F/C on 100s for Brst and Fly RI or on times
4. 20 × 50 F/C, every third 'A' stroke, shirts and paddles for 1/15

Hypoxic work routines should now be well established, with water strength and endurance made greater through the use of shirts and/or tubes with paddles.

Speed is being gradually introduced now that a base of aerobic fitness has been established. There is emphasis on F/C and Fly to instil early levels of endurance, but as skill levels are established the coach can make use of I/M sets.

1. 400 F/C and 200 B/C W/U
2. 6 × 5 × 1 I/M, 'A' stroke × 2 on 2.30
3. 6 × S – K – P – S (swim, kick, pull, swim) 'A' stroke on 2/2.30
4. 15 mins grab to pike starts
5. 20 × 50 alt F/C and Fly with every 4th 'A'

1. 500 F/C and 200 B/C
2. 2 × 200 F/C with shirts and paddles hypoxic 5 on 2 2 × 400 F/C with shirts and paddles hypoxic 3 and 5 on 5.45 2 × 200 F/C hypoxic 5 on 2.30
3. Pull 2 × 150 'A' then swim 100 RI work Kick 4 × 100 'A' kick then 100 swim Swim and build 6 × 50 'A' on 50/70
4. Swim; turn and finish controlled breathing 50s

In these routines strength, endurance and lung efficiency are still being established, although they are now well enough developed to provide the stamina and controlled breathing work required in simulated race techniques. In front crawl, the coach could instruct 'push-offs', then four to six kicks and three pulls before breathing (but with no breathing in and out of turns and finishes).

Pre-Competitive

1. 800 F/C loosen swim and bilateral
2. 2 × 200 I/M on 3.30 2 × 400 I/M on 6 mins 2 × 200 I/M on 3.30
3. Pull 3 × 400 F/C and B/C on

5.50/6.20; Brst or Fly 4 × 200 on 3.40;
Fly can be one and one (1 Fly 1 F/C)
Kick 'A' 2 × 2 × 200 RI 15, then a 50
hard on 90 T.T. 60

4. Swim 'A' 2 × 2 × 300 technique swims
   RI 20 then 50 hard on 80; F/C or
   B/C... 2 × 2 × 150 technique swims
   and 50 hard on 90 for Brst and Fly

1. Flexibility and 800 loosen F/C
2. 12 × 100 'A'; F/C or B/C on 2 mins
   T.T. P.B. + 12
   8 × 100 Brst or Fly on 2.40   T.T. P.B.
   + 15, hold swim times
3. 800 drills own choice
4. 10 mins turn techniques
5. 10 × 50 'A' on 60

1. 800 W/U progressive stroking
2. 3 × 200 F/C on 2.30/2.45
   2/3 × a
   2 × 100 F/C on 80/90
   4 × 50 each 4 × 50 on 45/50/60
3. 3 × 400 F/C or B/C or 3 × 150 Brst or
   Fly RI work
4. Kick 10 × 50 alternating hard/easy on
   90/70

The above schedules will now indicate if
a satisfying level of fitness has been
reached. The 'pressed load' levels of
training and the swimmer's ability to
sustain enforced targets are all relative to
the pre-competitive period of development.

SPRINT TRAINING

(Competitive)
Any training is specific and is, of course,
completed in the necessary stages before
competition. Sprint training will impose a
high level of anaerobic stress on the
swimmer because it is a period when
overload is injected into the programme;
this produces a satisfactory level of

speed, and the strength necessary to produce that speed. The physiological purpose of anaerobic training is:

• To develop the size of the fast-twitch
fibres in muscles, and possibly their
number.
• To make them come into play more
efficiently and quickly; in other words to
improve nerve/muscle co-ordination and
synchronization, when many fibres can
be called into use instantly, and extra
fibres as required.
• To increase the quantity and efficiency of anaerobic enzymes.

Although it is the competitive period, the
coach must be aware of the need to maintain a certain level of aerobic work. This
may be provided for in a long warm-up,
in technique swims and the occasional
easy distance swim at the beginning of a
schedule. Remember that each swimmer
has individual requirements so while one
might prefer a 1,500m/2,000m warm-up,
another is satisfied with 400m/800m.
   The dominant feature of this period,
however, is the programming of the
swimmer and the individual stroke to the
speeds necessary – although a level of
anaerobic threshold should be maintained. As we have stated earlier, the
faster a person moves in the water, the
greater the resistance that person creates
in obedience to the inverse square law:
thus as the swimmer doubles his speed,
the resistance is quadrupled, and if the
speed is quadrupled then the resistance is
increased sixteen-fold.
   Muscular strength uses high levels of
oxygenated energy and produces correspondingly high levels of lactic acid. The
result is a relatively high degree of stress
for the swimmer that he must learn to tolerate and overcome. It therefore becomes
necessary to increase the period of rest

between swims so the body can recover to some extent. Weight training goes a considerable way to providing an improved level of strength, although it is important that this is coupled with very good technical skill, because only then will a swimmer be able to keep an efficient 'fix' on the water. This will gain maximum propulsion for the speed of the stroke in question. Remember that each stroke employs different muscle patterns; it would be pointless, therefore, for a breaststroker to swim an anaerobic set on front crawl.

By following a logical routine the energy systems respond by becoming even more efficient. Thus in this final stage of preparation, the body is tapered and peaked, ready for competition.

Early Competitive
(Threshold and anaerobic systems)

Descending Set
1. 10 mins flexibility and 800 loosening F/C
2. Brst and Fly 600 own choice drills pulling and kicking
    F/C and B/C 1200 own choice drills (target time swims)
3. Brst and Fly are the lower set:
    3/4 × 100 on 1.50 P.B. + 14
    3/4 × 100 on 2 mins descend by 2 secs and hold
    3/4 × 100 on 2.15 hold set on previous set times
4. Easy 400 S/D

Distance Swimmer
1. Flexibility and 800 loosen F/C
2. 12 × 50 F/C on 60/70 easy hard H.P.R. 180 (an. thr.)
    3 × 200 timed swims and 800 F/C linked swim on average of 200 times (H.P.R. 180)
3. 800 technique set own choice drills

1. 800 loosen swim bilateral F/C
2. Interval rest ascending swims:
    8/12 × 100 'A' on 2 mins/2.20 T.T. P.B. 14 for every second gained under T.T. then increase 'on time' by 15 secs
3. 5 × 100 kick 'A' on 2.30 T.T. 1.45
    Pull 4 × 75/150 'A' RI 30 Swim
    8 × 50/75 1 easy, 1 hard
4. 8 × 25 progressive swims on 50
    400 S/D

Distance Swim
1. Easy 800 loosen
2. Swim 15 × 100 F/C on 2.15 at 1,500m pace
    1 × 500 at 1,500m pace (An. Thr.)
3. 800 drills

Competitive

(Anaerobic lactate and ATP – CP systems)

The types of swim a coach might use during this period would be:

*   Descending/reducing and progressive sets.
*   Negative splits, where the second part of the swim is faster than the first part.
*   Race simulators and sprint training.
*   Broken and high quality repetitions.
*   Fast interval training

1. 600 easy F/C W/U
2. Brst/Fly: swim 2 × broken 200s RI 10 secs at the 50s and 3 mins at the 200s
    F/C and B/C: swim 8 × 100 from a dive on 5 mins
3. 600 drills 'A'
4. Swim 6 × 50 'A' from a dive on 2 mins

400m (freestyle) swimmers (a.m.).

1. 800 loosening swim
2. Swim 4 × 200 time-holding swims RI 2 to 3 mins
    3 × 400 time-holding swims RI 2 to 3 mins

3. Kick 3 × 150 easy and 50 hard RI 30
    Pull 4 × 200 'building' swims pull
    buoy and rubber band RI 60
4. 8 × 50 F/C alternate hard/easy on 1.45

400m (freestyle) swimmers (p.m.).

1. 600/800 loosening swim
2. 400 easy kick and pull
3. Warm-up 50s then 25s hard on 90
    4 × 100 P.B. + 10 on 4 mins S/D 200
    Swim 3 × 50 hard from a dive on 2 mins
    Swim 5 × 25s from a dive then 400 S/D

THE TAPER

An American coach was once quoted as saying, 'It takes a lot of guts to taper'. There is a certain amount of truth in this statement, but more important still in this respect is the rapport between the swimmer and coach; knowing how his athlete ticks is vital for any coach.

If a swimmer has experienced a heavy build-up in his training programme, a degree of anxiety tends to creep in as the work load decreases. However, the taper is a vital necessity in any programme and the swimmer should feel no tiredness or muscle ache at the end of it, but rather, should be full of confidence for the forthcoming competition. It is essential to have achieved pace in any competitive programme, and during the taper period great emphasis must still be placed on it in the schedules; it is as important to the sprinter as it is to the distance swimmer. Depending on the amount of training and the water time available, any taper should take from seven to fourteen days. Counsilman was head coach to the American team in the Montreal Olympics and created a three-week taper. Many said he was wrong, but the results they achieved completely vindicated his judgement.

A taper is a scaling down of the work levels, so how is this accomplished? One way would be to phase out the morning sessions and just train in the afternoons; another would be to train one day and rest the next. Whatever is decided upon, the levels of strength and fitness must remain constant during this period for the peak to occur on the day of competition. The taper can cover many forms, each one important and relative to the competition it applies to at the time. In Chapter 9, cyclical training methods were explained in detail. A micro-cycle of training may cater for the vast number of weekend meets that fill our competitive calender. The most important meets throughout the year must be the Short and Long Course Championships. Other meets that take place during the preparation for these championships must be avoided or 'swum through' without the benefit of any 'easing off' in the training programme. The whole concept of the taper not only means reducing the training load, it also means concentrating on the quality of your work and improving your technique. The micro taper is necessary as it assesses the progress of the swimmer or squad.

One aspect of meets spent away that is seldom considered with enough care, is the quality of the accommodation. Is it near the centre of the competition? Keep the more garrulous members of the squad to separate rooms. Other aspects should be considered, too, such as food quality and quantity, and the restaurant opening times.

A number of schedules are outlined here:

1. Swim 600 or as required
2. 8 × 25s: 1 to 4 warming up, then 5 to 8 sprints
3. Pace 3 × 50 from a dive on the pace

the swimmer wants to hit on the way through the swim

4. Starts and turns for 20 mins
5. 500 easy kick and pull own choice drills

1. 400 to 800 loosening, warm-up swim
2. Swim 4 × 100 on 4 mins
3. Kick easy/hard 200 Pull easy/hard 200 Flyers one and one
4. Swim 4 × 25, then 4 × 50 RI 3 mins, or coach talk-back; all swims relate to race pace
5. S/D easy 300

1. 10 mins stretching, then 400/600 W/U
2. 12 × 50 from moderate to progressive speed
3. Kick 200, then 4 × 50 hard on 90 Pull 2 × 200/100, then 4 × 50 hard on 90/145
4. 2 × 100 negative split swims, long rest
   6 × 25 all-out sprint, then 400 S/D.

1. Swim 500 loosen
2. 400 S – K – P – S, then swim 6 × 50 steady build
3. 20 mins starts and turns
4. Swim 8 × 50 from a dive, long rest
5. Swim 6 × 25s from a dive, 'feed-back' RI
6. 300 S/D

Early Taper

(Distance swimmer, involving long warm-up and pace swims.)

1. 800/1,500 inclusive of kicking and pulling
2. 500 getting pace for the 1,500
   250 getting pace right for the 500
   125 getting the pace right for the 250
   2 × 25 getting pace for the 125
3. Long swim down

A seven-day taper may take the following form:

Monday	5,500m to 6,000m aerobic and anaerobic threshold work.
Tuesday	Maintaining the conditioning with aerobic work and anaerobic sets with either broken swims, or descending and negative splits. The yardage is reduced with longer rests built into the schedules.
Wednesday	Long warm-up, with kicking and pulling on the 'A' stroke. 'Power' swimming over 20m with push-offs. Starts, turns and squad take-over techniques. 3,000m to 4,000m.
Thursday	Training p.m. only, with long warm-up. A 'simulator', with analysis on all major techniques. Broken swim/s to iron out assessed faults from simulator. Long swim-down.
Friday	Training p.m. with a long warm-up. Easy kicking and pulling on 'A' stroke, dive start swims 25m, then a 50m swim/s with turns.
Saturday	Training p.m., with long warm-up and swims concentrating on building technique. Working on all known weaknesses with or without 'stress' sprints over short distances. Long swim-down.
Sunday	Rest day: competition on Monday, Tuesday, Wednesday.

INDIVIDUAL MEDLEY SWIMMING

If the swimmers in any one group were asked what their 'A' or first stroke was, coupled with the event in question, very few would indicate the individual medley. It involves swimming all the competitive strokes, and therefore the swimmer must condition for each of these strokes in training. In the preparation period – and indeed for other periods – the individual medley is a great asset to the programme for conditioning the swimmer. If we consider the triathlon event, the athlete is most likely to improve his time by improving the slower discipline. Thus in the individual medley the greatest gain in time will relate to improving the two slower strokes, namely the breaststroke and backstroke sections. A good I/M swimmer is proficient on all strokes, and has the confidence to switch efficiently from stroke to stroke; the difficulties will lie with the swimmer who is only proficient in one or two strokes.

A swimmer expends a great deal of oxygenated energy on a stroke or strokes in which he or she is not efficiently proficient, and the coach must take this into consideration as he counsels the swimmer either to go hard on the weaker strokes and stroke the strong ones, or vice versa. Derry O'Rourke (as Irish National coach), had a very good analogy for the medley event. This stated that if two swimmers swam the 400m individual medley event and both their times were the same, it indicated that either the pace was wrong, or that each swimmer had strengths in the different strokes. The example was as shown below.

The event was obviously a men's 400m I/M, and swimmer 'A' paced it better than swimmer 'B'. However, swimmer 'B' may have gone hard on the butterfly section, because his breaststroke was the weak stroke. The 'advice to the swimmer' is superb with a swimmer who is proficient on all four strokes; the same advice could also be adopted for the perfect 400m front crawl race.

The 100m I/M event should pose no problems for the conditioned swimmer. The problems multiply, however, for the 200m I/M event, and become greater still in the 400m I/M event. The turn in this event which has caused many problems in the past is the back-to-breast turn; all the others should pose no problems. The coach must remember that the swimmer is out of oxygen for anything up to four seconds when he performs the back-to-breast turn. What is more, I/M swimmers often negate the breaststroke 'pull-out' (back to the costume) and go instead for the shorter arm cycle during this phase.

	Swimmer 'A'	Swimmer 'B'	Advice to swimmer
Butterfly	1.07	1.00	Smooth
Back crawl	1.09	1.10	Pick-up
Breaststroke	1.18	1.22	Work
Front crawl	1.06	1.08	Kick home
	4.40 secs	4.40 secs	

The reverse somersault turn is slow and increases the oxygen debt factor even more. The best procedure would seem to be a 'Naber' head-up type back-turn with a fast spin onto the breast position ('spin-over' turn, see Chapter 7); this enables a 'late' oxygen inhalation with a faster transition into the breaststroke leg action. The complexities are many, and coaches often opt out by giving straight sets instead of concentrating on the prevalent weaknesses. But there are umpteen opportunities for creating interest and enthusiasm here, and it always comes as a surprise to me that this method of training the swimmer isn't used to a greater degree.

In the following examples the first few are straight I/M sets with variations to the distance and order of swimming the strokes. Various components and different types of normal training procedures can be introduced which will enhance the sets still more. All times and swims given here relate to a 25m 6-lane pool.

EXAMPLES OF INDIVIDUAL MEDLEY SETS

1. Normal I/M set:
   1 × 4 × 1 I/M on 2.15
   (25 Fly – 25 B/C – 25 Brst – 25 F/C)
   Kick 400 I/M order

2. Reverse I/M set:
   1 × 4 × 1 I/M on 2.15
   (25 F/C – 25 Brst – 25 B/C – 25 Fly)

3. Straight and reverse set (back to back):
   2 × 4 × 1 I/M on 2.15
   First set straight, then reverse order

4. Any other stroke which was thought weak can now be added to the set eg breaststroke:
   1 × 5 × 1 on 2.45
   (25 Fly – 25 B/C – 50 Brst – 25 F/C)

5. A stroke may even be omitted for a specific reason.
   1 × 3 × 1 on 90
   (25 Fly – 25 B/C – 25 F/C)

6. You can inject an easy or hard leg of any stroke between the normal I/M:
   50 Fly and 25 F/C – 50 B/C and 25 F/C – 50 Brst and 25 F/C – 50 F/C and 25 easy

7. Pyramid set
   1 Fly – 1 B/C – 1 Brst – 1 F/C on 2.10
   2 Fly – 2 B/C – 2 Brst – 2 F/C on 3.50
   3 Fly – 3 B/C – 3 Brst – 3 F/C on 6.45
   4 Fly – 4 B/C – 4 Brst – 4 F/C on 9 min
   3 Fly – 3 B/C – 3 Brst – 3 F/C
   2 Fly – 2 B/C – 2 Brst – 2 F/C
   1 Fly – 1 B/C – 1 Brst – 1 F/C

The same pyramid set could have a 400 F/C swim introduced instead of the 4 Fly – 4 B/C – 4 Brst – 4 F/C; again, the set could be interspersed with a 25 F/C at various parts of the set. The variations are many.

8. Hungarian set:
   8 × 25 Fly on 40
   4 × 50 B/C on 70
   2 × 100 Brst on 2.20
   1 × 200 F/C hypoxic 3 and 5 on 3 mins
   2 × 100 Fly on 2.20
   4 × 50 B/C on 70
   8 × 25 – 4 Brst and 4 F/C

The formula on this Hungarian set can be changed as you wish to give contrast and interest to the swimmer. The times could be slower on the way up and faster on the way down. The hypoxic routine was added to increase overload.

9. You can use a broken length I/M, with the stroke changing halfway. Another interesting method is 4 × 3 × 1 I/Ms. Swimmers line up one behind the other, go up one lane, duck under the

lane rope into the next. Three lanes are used for each group, with the fourth stroke being the 'lead off' stroke after every set:

Fly – B/C – Brst
F/C – Fly – B/C
Brst – F/C – Fly
B/C – Brst – F/C

RACE PLANNING ———————————

Every swimmer should have a race plan, and this should be uppermost in mind just before the race. If the swimmer is swimming a 100m front crawl event, decisions during the event must be made about the following:

- The entry must be streamlined.
- After the start, how many kicking cycles should take place before surfacing?
- How many surface stroke cycles should take place before oxygen inhalation?
- How many kicking cycles/arm cycles off the wall before breathing?

EXAMPLE OF A SCHEDULE LAYOUT FOR A COACHING COURSE ———————

Late Pre-Competitive

		Endurance	
		Skill	Speed
Water time 1.5 hours, 25m pool		Distance	Time
1. 400/600 F/C loosening W/U		600m	8 mins
Main section (front crawl)			
2. 3 × 4 × 75 on 75 An. Thr. H.P.R. 180 2 × 4 × 100 on 90 and 1 min 20s An Thr. – H.P.R. 180 S/D 200 easy		1,900m	25 mins
Sectional work ('A' stroke) no RI more than 20 secs			
3. Kick 2 × 200 then 4 x 50 hard Pull 2 × 400 F/C or B/C or Brst and Fly 5 × 100		1,400m	22 mins
Turns ('A' stroke and flip turn)			
4. 15 mins ('A' stroke and flip turn)			15 mins
Lactate tolerance sprints			
5. 10 × 50 F/C (every 3rd 'A') on 90 H.P.R. 190/200 S/D 400 easy		900m	20 mins
		Total: 4,800m	1.5 hrs

Coach.......................

- What should the splits be on the 25, 50 and 75?
- What breathing cycle should be applied during the race and the final 10–15m?

The plan has many variants, with each aspect as important as another one. The plan can be formulated during the taper period with each stroke having similar objectives. The fundamentals are logical and require establishing in a chronological order. Page 162 gives an example of a schedule layout which could be used for a coaches' course. The schedule is concise, in order to show knowledge and balance of the various components.

TRAINING SCHEDULES OF SOME PROMINENT IRISH SWIMMERS AND COACHES

Derry O'Rourke

Former Irish National Coach and King's Hospital School A.S.C. (Leinster Province).

Swimmers:
Miriam Hopkins, 1976 Olympics (Montreal), ASA 200 butterfly champion 2.19.28.
Catherine Bohan, 1980 Olympics (Moscow), ASA breaststroke champion 2.37.50.
Michelle Smith, 1988 (Seoul) and 1992 (Barcelona) Olympics, ASA 200 backstroke champion 2.14.41; European and World Champion on 200 Fly and 200 I/M 1995.

Preparation Period (25m pool)

1. 1,000 mixed W/U full stroke and drills
2. 3 × 5 × 100 F/C RI 30 – 4 + 1 (4 pulse

rate 150, 1 pulse rate 120) then 200 B/C after every 5th swim
3. 6 × 100 I/M kick (no board) and sculling drills with hands on 2.30
4. 20 × 50 I/M order on 60
5. 200 Brst streamlining, 1 pull 2 kicks (second kick submerged and streamlined)
6. 12 × 25 F/C slow fast on 60

Pre-Competitive

1. 12 × 100 F/C W/U – 4 on 90 – 4 on 85 – 4 on 80
2. 200 drills:
   8 × 100 Fly on 90
   8 × 100 B/C on 90
   8 × 100 Brst on 90
   8 × 100 F/C on 90 then 200 easy F/C
3. 3 × 200 kick descending on 4 mins
   2 × 3 × 200 pull on 3 mins (each set descending)
   own choice, then 200 drills (all I/M)
4. 3 × 200 kick descending on 4 mins
   2 × 3 × 200 pull on 3 mins (each set descending) then 200 drills
5. 20 × 50 F/C on 40 then 200 S/D

Paddy Hayes

Former coach to Borough of South Tyneside A.S.C and Trojan A.S.C. (Leinster Province).

Swimmers:
Kevin Boyd (doctor), British record holder (see below).
Ian Wilson, British 1,500m record holder.
Lyn Wilson, 1988 Olympics: 200m butterfly.
Cathy White, 1984 Olympics: 100m and 200m backstroke.

Kevin Boyd was the first British swimmer to break 15 min in the 1,500m freestyle, in a new British record time of 14 mins 57 secs (short course) in the

Europo Cup, Edinburgh 1988. He came 4th in the 400m freestyle event at the World Championships in Madrid in 1986 with a time of 3.51.09, and was 7th in the 1,500m at the 1988 Olympics (15 mins 17 secs) where he broke the Olympic record in the heats. He held seven Commonwealth records, seventeen British records and twenty-one English records.

Pre-Competitive (25m pool)

1. 8 × 50 F/C descending
2. 2 × 5 × 75 on 55 T.T. 43.5/45
   2 × 8 × 50 on 35 T.T. 26/27.5
   2 × 4 × 100 on 70 T.T. 57/58.5
   2 × 2 × 200 on 2.30 T.T. 2 mins
   16 × 25 on 20 T.T. 12.5/13
   16 × 25 on 30 T.T. 17/20
   400 F/C timed T.T. 3.53/3.55
   16 × 25 on 30 T.T. 20
3. 10 × 200 on 2.30 T.T. 2.05/2.10
4. 20 mins swim and drill

Competitive

On Friday he swam in the Monte Carlo Meet and came first in the 1,500m event, when he broke the 1,500m British record in a time of 15 mins 22 secs. He also won the 400m in 3 mins 52 secs and the 200m in 1 mins 52 secs. On the Tuesday before this he trained in a 33⅓yd pool as follows:

1. 8 × 2 lengths F/C descending
2. 800 F/C on 8 mins T.T. 7.49
   7 × 100 on 65 T.T. 53/54
   400 easy swim
   9 × 400s on 5 mins T.T. 3.55
3. 20 mins swim and drills

Taper

Kevin worked on a ten-day taper, reducing yardage and intensity.

1. 2–3,000 warm-up session swimming all strokes
2. 8 × 50 on 35 descending to race pace
3. 2–3,000m S/D

When Kevin did two sessions a day he covered 84,000m a week. When he trained three sessions a day he covered 130,000m a week.

Bobby Madine

Coach to Leander A.S.C. (Ulster Province)

Swimmer

Marion Madine (law student Queen's University Belfast);
Irish National Champion and English Open National Champion.

Best Times:

Butterfly	Long Course	Short Course
50m	29.26	28.90
100m	1.03.27	1.02.20
200m	2.15.95	2.13.90

Basal pulse rate 40

Preparation Period

Training comprises one session a day 0600 to 0800 Monday to Saturday. After the first week, all training was based on lactate testing, using Analox GM7 unit. Four weeks of land conditioning commenced prior to the first week of the season.

1. 15 × 200 F/C pull on 3 mins (or RI 10 secs if using tube + paddles)
2. 24 – 22 – 20 × 50 kick on 50/55/60 secs (choice)
3. 10 × 25 swim on 60
4. 3 × 500 F/C on 7.30
5. 15 × 100 F/C RI 10 secs

Total = 7,250m

The following training times were produced on computer from a programme developed by Bobby Madine:

Pre-Competitive

1. 500 pull 300 kick 200 swim
2. 1 × 400 F/C kick (lactate 1.5) RI 30
3. 3 × 200 F/C kick A.T. RI 30
4. 8 × 25 O/C on 75
5. 4 × 50 O/C on 90
6. 1 × 400 F/C (lactate 2) RI 10
      a 2 × 200 O/C (lactate 2) RI 30
      3 ×
      a 2 × 200 O/C (lactate 2) RI 10
7. 5 × 200 pull tube and paddles RI 10
8. 1 × 200 S/D stroke drills

     Total = 7,000m

Taper

(Last week)

Monday	I maintain the distance at 6,000/6,500m but reduce the intensity from anaerobic threshold levels at the beginning of the week.
Tuesday	All aerobic maintenance work on lactates 1.5/2.0 inclusive of 25m sprints.
Wednesday	Aerobic maintenance all at lactate level 1.5. Include 50m sprints with dive starts and turns. Back crawl flags up at all sessions.
Thursday	Rest day

Friday, Saturday, Sunday: competition

David McCullagh

Coach to Templeogue A.S.C. (Leinster Province).

Swimmer:

Valerie Russell. After obtaining the Leaving Certificate, Valerie won a four-year scholarship at West Virginia University. Irish international and record holder: Irish National Champion on the 50m, 100m, 200m back crawl and 200m individual medley. A.S.A. Age Group Champion for 1992 and 1993.

Best Times:

	Back Crawl	Individual Medley	
50m	30.9	200m	2.24.55
100m	1.05.02	400m	5.03.95
200m	2.19.96		

As it was Valerie's final school year, planning had to take into account the fact that her swimming programme would be affected due to academic pressures. Heavy training formed the bulk of work from September to January including a three-week camp in Florida. The following schedules are some samples of this phase in the programme. They involve a back crawl week which was usually followed by an individual medley week, and following this a week of both back crawl and individual medley. Much of the work is based on 'percentages' of her PB and on pulse rates.

Thursday a.m. (05.20)

1. Weights session
2. 1 × 400 reverse I/M
      10 × 50 I/M order on 45
3. 4 × 400 B/C on 5.40 (an. thresh.)
      1 × 200 Brst kick
4. 2 × 8 x 100 B/C on 80 (an thresh.)
      1 × 200 Brst kick
5. 2 × 50 B/C sprints on 3 mins
      1 × 200 F/C S/D

Friday a.m. (05.20)

1. 100 B/C kick and 100 supine Fly kick
   100 RA and 100 LA then 100 full stroke
   B/C
2. 5 × (2 × 50 B/C kick on 60; 2 × 50 Fly kick on 70)
3. 3 × 800 B/C on 11 mins (An. Thresh.)

200 Brst pull and 200 kick
4. 3 × (50 B/C on 2 mins; 2 × 25 B/C on 60) sprint set (95% on the 50s and 98.5% on the 25s)
5. 200 F/C medium-pace S/D

Saturday a.m. 07.30
1. Weights
2. 1 × 400 reverse I/M
3. 30 × 50 B/C on 40 T.T. 38 (an. thresh. 75%)
4. 200 Fly kick; 200 single arm Fly
5. 5 × 200 B/C on 6 mins T.T. 2.30 (lac tol 93%) 200 F/C; 200 Brst; 200 Fly
6. 20 × 75 B/C on 60 (an. thresh.)
7. 6 × 25B/C on 60, then 200 S/D

Sunday a.m. 09.00
1. 800 F/C build
2. 10 × 200 B/C on 2.45 T.T. 2.40 (an. thresh. 85%)
3. 2 × (100 B/C kick and 100 supine Fly kick)
4. 3 × 3 × 100 B/C on 2.30 (93%)
5. 10 × 50 F/C on 50
6. Fly set 3 × 200 on 3.10; 3 × 100 on 1.35; 3 × 50 on 45
7. 300 S/D

Valerie had some difficulty in achieving the 50 split on the 100 B/C. To improve this, we worked on long rest 50s and some 25s. We also worked on starts and turns with 15-mins extra sessions across widths of the pool. Because of her academic commitments, a large proportion of the workouts were centred on anaerobic and pace work. This was successful due to the extensive background of endurance and aerobic work accomplished early on in the season.

The taper work focused on simulators, broken swims and maintaining the aerobic conditioning. The weekly distance decreased on a diminishing basis from 40,000m to 15,000m with emphasis on flexibility and relaxation techniques.

The year's programme was successful – as the results testified – at both the Irish and the English ASA Championships.

Kevin Williamson

Coach to Terenure ASC (Leinster Branch). Double Olympian Montreal 1976 and Moscow 1990. Awarded a BSc degree at the University of Michigan.' Big Ten' gold medallist relay.

Swimmers:
Aibne Bergin, Irish Champion 50m and 100m front crawl.

Best Times:	Front Crawl
50m	23.43
100m	51.44

Mark Battelle, Irish Champion 50m, 200m and 400m front crawl.

Best Times:	Front Crawl
50m	23.50
200m	1.50.20
400	3.55.40

During heavy training the programme consisted of four morning sessions, each day from 06.15 until 07.45, and six afternoon two-hour sessions consisting of alternating between weights and running for 45 to 75 mins, then 75 mins in the water. The weekly maximum was 50,000m and the average swimming was 35,000m per week.

Kevin worked on three phases for the year and tapered accordingly for December, March and July. His coaching plan revolves around two main themes in the annual programme, building and descending.

'Building' is the ability to build a strength factor throughout the complete propulsive phase of the stroke. It also entails the will-power and lung capacity to hold a long underwater phase in any stroke in both the start and particularly the turn. 'Descending' is when the swimmer can build and maintain pace, then negatively split the second half of the race.

During the first phase of training Kevin placed great emphasis on stroke technique and building the above themes and skills into the programme. Each of the schedules reflects the programme themes.

Saturday 14.30 to 16.30
Preparation (25m pool)

1. 3×400 F/C swim, pull, kick and a 400 I/M
2. $4 \times 3 \times 50$ on 60 kick, drill, full stroke with Fly, B/C, Brst, F/C
3. $6 \times 6 \times 4 \times 1$ I/M on 2 mins
4. Drills and full stroke on 'A' stroke; 4×150 kick on 3 mins; 5×200 pull on 2.45; 6×300 on 4.30 descend
5. 6×25 dive 1 length underwater swims; 200 S/D

Saturday 14.30 to 16.30
Pre-competitive

1. 1×800 F/C W/U
2. 10×75 pull RI 60; 6×100 kick on 2 mins
3. 4×75 kick on 90; 6×50 kick on 60 3rd and 6th hard
   8×25 kick on 45 1–3 easy and 4–6 hard
4. 8×25 underwater swims on 50
   3×50 pace swims for the next 'holding' pace set

This set accentuates the 'building' and 'descending' theme
5×100 on 75 holding 68
4×200 on 2.25 holding 2.16
3×300 on 3.35 holding 3.24
2×400 on 4.45 holding 4.32
1×500 L.T. time trial coming back hard
Long S/D

Ger Doyle

Coach to New Ross ASC (Leinster Province)

Swimmers:
Adrian O'Connor, age 21, Honours degree in Electronics at Waterford RTC Irish champion and record holder in the 50m, 100m and 200m back crawl.

Best Times:
50m   26.17
100m   55.23
200m   2.00.45

Niamh O'Connor, age 20, Business Studies at Waterford RTC Irish record holder 50m and 100m back crawl.

Best Times:
50m   29.44
100m   1.02.4

Hugh O'Connor, age 14 Youth Olympic gold and bronze medallist 100m and 200m back crawl; Junior 100m Irish Champion.

Best Times:
50m   28.39
100m   59.89
200m   2.12.38

Ger's programme is built around quality rather than quantity with a great deal of emphasis on stroke technique. All sessions are varied, and each lasts for no more than 1 h 15 mins.

Sample sessions:

800 mixed W/U
12×50 kick F/C alt B/C on 60
10×100 No 1 on 1.10/1.15
200 easy swim
4×100 I/M pull on 1.30

3 × 4 × 50 F/C on 40
200 S/D

Pyramid W/U 2 × (50, 100, 15, 200) alt F/C and B/C
8 × 50 I/M order kick on 60
18 × 50 No 1 on 40/45 (4 × 4 × PRO)
200 easy swim
8 × 50 pull No 2 stroke on 50
4 × 200 (2 × F/C, 2 × No 1) on 2.20/2.30 to 2.40
100 easy swim
4 × 25 under-water sprint kick on 60
200 S/D

IN CONCLUSION

The programmes and schedules provided here are unique and full of interest, and they all show the individual flair of each coach in relation to the swimmers on the squad. The many types of swim, with all their varying components and an emphasis on the physiological concepts, are included in their different forms. (The technical details are covered in earlier chapters in the book.) The author is obliged to all the coaches for taking the time and trouble in compiling each of the programmes.

Index